PLAYING LIVING LEARNING

A Worldwide Perspective on Children's Opportunities to Play

Cor Westland
Jane Knight

Published by
Venture Publishing, Inc.
1640 Oxford Circle
State College, Pa. 16801
U.S.A.

Designed and typeset by
A.P.H. Limited, 1050 Baxter Road Ottawa, Ontario

Library of Congress Card
No. 81 69902

Preface

Within the covers of this book you will find one of the most comprehensive studies yet assembled on the various comparative forms and patterns of children's play around the world. The World Leisure and Recreation Association, which is composed of recreation professionals and others interested in enhancing human growth and development through leisure opportunities, believes very strongly that the degree of richness of children's play is one of the critical factors which determine the future quality of their lives.

Since Piaget, who was the first scientist to demonstrate the principle that the variety and quality of play experiences is very important for the mental, physical and psychological development of children, others have retested and reproven that principle. Many of us now believe that each child's individual development potential can be severely limited by inadequate play experiences at early ages. What is now also realized by many people is that the sum total of the development of all children in a society is one of the major determinants of the level of social and economic development which that society can achieve.

Yet today we face the problem in the industrialized and developing countries alike, of eroding opportunities for these essential play experiences. The reduction in government funds for social pograms in industrialized countries, and the ever rising population of children in most developing countries, will have serious effects on future generations if the present trend continues for very long.

Those who labor with dedication against this eroding tide deserve our gratitude and our support. The World Leisure and Recreation Association is very pleased to present this, its first published book, for their use, and to dedicate it to them.

In so doing we wish to acknowledge with grateful appreciation the support and services of Dr. Aldaba-Lim and the staff of the International Year of the Child, who encouraged WLRA to make this study as part of its efforts for the International Year of the Child, and who made their communications network available to us.

i

We also wish to thank UNICEF whose staff assisted with the identification of appropriate agencies around the world, the Canadian Parks/ Recreation Association which provided most valuable administrative assistance throughout the formative stages of this project, and who was instrumental in securing a generous financial contribution from the Government of Canada which made the compilation and preparation possible. We also want to acknowledge the assistance received from the International Association for the Child's Right to Play which placed its considerable resource network at our disposal.

All of us however are indebted mostly to Cor Westland and Jane Knight who labored in their leisure time to assemble, study, organize, and write the work we proudly present to you, the reader.

Robert O. Wilder
Chairman of the Board of the
World Leisure and Recreation Association

Table of Contents

Introduction

W hen the late William D. Cunningham, Executive Director of the World Leisure and Recreation Association, recommended that a Compendium of the most imaginative play programs be put together as a tribute to the International Year of the Child (IYC), nobody could foresee that this rather simple and straight-forward idea would acquire dimensions far beyond the original thought.

As soon as we started researching the project, it became clear that a simple listing of programs would not do justice to the widely varying applications of specific concepts around the world. Such an enumeration would do little to deepen the understanding of the impact of cultural differences on play and the provision of play opportunities; but above all, such a treatment would fail to show that play and the issues surrounding it are not limited by socio-economic conditions, or by levels of technological development, but are worldwide concerns, increasingly preoccupying people, wherever they live.

At the same time, because of the universality of certain solutions, we felt that we would have to provide sufficient detail and reference material to enable their application if desirable.

Therefore, upon consultation with the World Leisure and Recreation Association, the sponsoring agency, we decided to broaden the scope of the book rather significantly, dropping the original idea of a compendium and instead providing a worldwide overview of programs aimed at improving children's opportunity to play. The intent was to group the various programs into specific categories, to show the various solutions groups in different countries have adopted to solve generally comparable problems. We have attempted to provide sufficient detail for a clear understanding of the respective projects, without using the case history method. We, furthermore, decided to include sufficient references, including both technical information and addresses of sponsoring agencies, so that our readers, if they should desire, would have no difficulties establishing further contacts.

The methodology followed was simple in set-up but complex in application. The first phase consisted of a questionnaire which, through the good offices of UNICEF, was sent to all National IYC Commissions. We hoped that this questionnaire would provide us with some basic data, the beginning of some form of categorization, and some insight into the possibilities of universal treatment of the various projects. This we followed up by corresponding with a large number of people and agencies, using the communications networks of the World Leisure and Recreation Association and the International Association for the Child's Right to Play. Finally, we established many personal contacts and made a large number of site visits.

All this took place over a period of two years. During that time, we received a large variety of material. Some agencies sent us extremely well-prepared reports; others limited their information to the questionnaire. A large number ignored the questionnaire but wrote us extensive letters; many sent pictures, slides, even films and videotapes; and from a number of projects we received nothing more than a folder or a newspaper article. Finally, we learned of others through the literature.

All told we received news of 184 projects and programs, originating in 37 countries. A number of projects are probably discontinued at the time of printing of the book. It has, for understandable reasons, been impossible to verify this. And, since we felt that whether or not a given project was still operational was less important than its concept and content, we decided therefore to report on all those that appeared relevant and interesting.

While analyzing the material, it became obvious that most of the programs fell into clearly identifiable categories, such as Toy Libraries, Adventure Play, and Playstreets. Others had features that placed them in several categories, such as the Mobile Play programs, those dealing with Nature, or the ones stressing Play and the Family. In these cases, we attempted to identify the dominant aspects of a program and categorized them on that basis.

Thus, we arrived at nine "theme chapters". Because of the multi-facetted aspects of a good many of the programs, this categorization is somewhat arbitrary; however, we considered this approach necessary to make comparisons possible and future reference easier.

Furthermore, although we felt that the book should be light on theory in view of the already abundant information in this area, we did include a few "conceptual chapters", because we wanted to explain certain aspects and principles in some detail to ensure continuity and clarity. For instance, we wanted to draw attention to the global and universal nature of play, and therefore of the opportunities to play. We thought that it might be helpful to highlight some of the societal issues that most directly effect children's opportunities to play and felt that a discussion of the various aspects of children's participation might increase understanding of this crucial issue.

After having dealt with the theme chapters, we added a chapter called "Reflections and Projections," in which we attempted to synthesize the most important aspects of these and identify some of the most important societal trends that will influence the provision of play opportunities as we see it.

As appendices we added a list of selected references which, for obvious reasons, does not claim to be comprehensive, but which may, nevertheless, be helpful to those who want to pursue more specialized study. We also listed the organizations that initiated and operate the programs that were discussed and the persons or agencies that can be contacted for future reference.

Although the book deals with all age groups, and wherever appropriate, stresses the importance of intergenerational contacts, the emphasis lies on the 6- to 12-year-old category. The scope of the material was kept as general and broad as practicality would permit. Our ability to work in six different language groups enabled us to use original material from a wide variety of countries.

The treatment of the various projects is solution rather than problem-orientated; in other words, although issues and challenges are identified, we did not go extensively into the causes of the problems to be solved, but rather presented some of the attempted solutions. We did not adopt a specific position as far as programs for the handicapped are concerned, and did not take sides in the issue of integration (main-streaming) or segregation, but rather presented the projects as they were developed. Therefore, a number of projects highlight an integrated approach, whereas others deal with handicapped children as a special group, with special needs, requiring special opportunities.

As the title of the book indicates the emphasis is on the total development of the child, stressing the strong interrelationship of playing, living, and learning, and the intent is to demonstrate this by dealing with the subject matter on a global scale.

That such an approach has limitations is obvious. For instance, in spite of serious efforts, it has not been possible to report on all world regions on an equal basis. Mail services are not of universal quality, political conditions make certain countries virtually inaccessible and, especially in most of the developing world, documented material on children's play programs is extremely scarce or simply non-existent. Therefore, our coverage is of necessity incomplete and a number of undoubtedly interesting and important projects had to be left out. Hopefully, a future edition of this book will rectify this weakness and produce a really comprehensive treatment.

One of the consequences of relying primarily on printed information is that most of the programs presented originate in the industrialized part of the world. On the other hand, one might argue that it is in these countries that the problems related to play and play spaces are most acutely felt.

The fact that both authors originate from highly industrialized societies, albeit from different cultural and linguistic environments, has undoubtedly influenced the treatment and approach, and may have resulted in insufficient emphasis on cultural and conceptual variations. This, plus the scarcity of material from the Third World, has undoubtedly caused insufficient attention to the special problems of these countries, especially in their rural areas. And, finally, the unavoidable gaps in coverage make the amount of reference material not as rich as it might be.

The book is directed to all those interested in children. We hope that it will be of interest and use to teachers, students, planners, recreation professionals, youth leaders as well as government and private agencies and the general public. Care has therefore been taken to write the book in easily flowing style, devoid of a typical textbook approach, while at the same time providing sufficient detail and data to interest the academic.

The over-all aim is one of motivation and inspiration. We hope that the book will provide a forum for discussion between professionals, as well as politicians, students and interested lay people. But above all, we hope that the book will prove to be a positive tool in the worldwide struggle for recognition of the need of people of all ages, not just to play, but also to have the opportunities to play.

A Spanish edition is being prepared at this time and a French one will hopefully follow shortly.

Play Times

Playing, Living, Learning

Play: A Global Concern

J ohan Huizinga, in his classic "Homo Ludens," reminds us that "play is more than a mere physiological or a psychological reflex."[1] It is a function of culture, one of the main bases of civilization, not associated with any particular stage of civilization, but a universal and integral part of all life, human as well as animal. Therefore, play is central not only to the development of children, but also to that of adults, and the community, and society.

As the International Association for the Child's Right to Play stated in its Malta Declaration in preparation for the International Year of the Child, "Play, along with the basic needs of nutrition, health, shelter and education, is vital for the development of the potential of all children."[2] Play is essential for their social, intellectual, emotional, creative and physical development. It is the element that provides them with the so often envied "joie de vivre". It teaches them lifelong skills and attitudes and serves as a natural and invaluable educational tool.

In the Western World, a growing amount of leisure and an increasing interest in the quality of life have brought into focus the importance of play for adults. The scarce quantities of free time industrial occupations allowed a number of years ago, could only serve to prepare adults for the demands of the work that was to follow. However, with the shortening of the workweek, a residue of free time began to appear that was increasingly used in playful exploits to change the pace, provide a break from the day-to-day routine and, more importantly, to refresh the mind, develop new and different social contacts and to acquire new skills.

For the community, play has become a vehicle for the development of a sense of neighbourhood, a feeling of belonging, of communication and therefore of unity. The play element knits a community together through the opportunities it provides for intergenerational contacts and multicultural appreciation and manifestations. Play has increasingly become the medium of respect for the natural environment; respect for people from different cultural and ethnic backgrounds; and, due to the fundamentally classless nature of play, respect for people as people and not as representatives of specific socio-economic strata with certain ascribed and traditional roles and privileges.

Society benefits from the play activities of its members through the overall climate play creates. If its members have learned to play individually and collectively, its dynamism and vitality will not be stifled and its creativity not suffocated in stereotyped models and constricting norms.

The focus of this book is on children and more in particular on their opportunities to play. Therefore, after these general observations, we will limit our discussions to them and point out a number of *myths or misconceptions* in relation to childrens' play.

● It is incorrect to assume that play is unimportant and frivolous, a mere passing of time, relaxation at best, but an activity we can well do without. On the contrary, play is an integral part of life itself; it is instructive, spontaneous and natural. Play for the child means exploring; it is communication and an important means of expression. In play, the child combines action and thought, and through play it finds satisfaction and a feeling of accomplishment. Therefore, play touches on all aspects of life; through play the child learns to live.

● The opposite of play for children is not work, as is often assumed, but boredom. Work, not in the context of child labour, is often play for a child. Through work, in the sense of commitment and serious application, the child feels useful, learns responsibility, develops emotionally, socially, mentally and physically.

● It is wrong to assume that providing for play means organizing a program. Rather, providing for play means making available the time, material, space, the proper atmosphere and playmates. All these are component parts of the opportunity to play and, with these, the children themselves take the initiative and create play situations. The notion that others, usually adults, have to organize programs for play to occur, eliminates the development of initiatives and responsibility and, more often than not, the real fun element. These are then replaced with adult-orientated rules and values which frequently hamper the development of a real play atmosphere.

● It is true that, given the opportunity, children will play anywhere and anytime; however, living in modern society has put severe limitations on these opportunities. We only have to look at the statistics of traffic accidents and incidences of vandalism to realize the consequences if appropriate conditions are not available.

Therefore, children must be provided with the opportunities to play in environments that are safe, without being sterile, and that provide sufficient challenges and occasions for participatory involvement to remove feelings of boredom and alienation which frequently lead to acts of vandalism.

Some of the *basic principles* to be kept in mind when dealing with play include the following:

- Play is a process and not primarily a product; one of the best examples of this is the adventure playground.
- Play covers the entire spectrum from informal to formal play, from structured to spontaneous activities and from serious involvement to sheer fun. Therefore, play is not stereotyped, not limiting but, on the contrary, touches life in all its facets.
- Play is to a large degree influenced by geography, climate, socio-economic conditions and cultural origins.

For instance, the issue of play spaces is probably more acute in the western world where children are to a large extent segregated from day-to-day life, than in other regions where they are an integral part of society. In the western cultures, children have their own part of the house and their own areas of town identified as play-areas. Play is localized in designated places and for specific times. When children are allowed in the adult world, it is under very special conditions. After all, it is the Anglo-Saxon world that devised the slogan "children should be seen but not heard", and it is not all that long ago that in certain countries children were required to stand when they ate in the presence of their elders.

What a difference from, for instance, the Indonesian culture where children are so totally a part of the over-all society that one meets them wherever one goes, under all circumstances. The world is indeed their playground, and, rather than being confined to a special part of the house, Indonesian children play in every part of it and share in every experience. Even the very young are being transported by the mother in the "slendang" wherever she goes.

In most cultures, opportunities to play are influenced by social tab-oos. For instance, after one has reached a certain age it is expected that one no longer plays certain games or participates in certain activities. This holds especially true for those societies that still have a definite social hierarchy. Intergenerational play is especially rare as a result. In striking contrast to this is play among the Inuit of Canada's Northland.In that society not only all ages participate in games, but this participation takes place at the same time and in the same game. All age groups, from small children to grandparents join in the game that is played for the joy and satisfaction of participation and not for the purpose of winning. A winner is rarely declared. The rules are there to suit the players and are therefore frequently changed.

It is important to realize that, in spite of those social and cultural differences, the quality of the various play experiences is not effected. It would be wrong to measure this according to the norms and standards one is accustomed to. Unfortunately, this still happens all too often. Children from different cultural back-grounds frequently have no choice but to fit in with the play activities that are prevalent in the society in which they have come to live, as a result of a lack of understanding of and appreciation for cultural differences on the part of those who are in a position of leadership.

In the past these attitudinal problems had few consequences because of the limited contacts between different societies. The increasing migration patterns however are introducing these issues into previously homogenious societies and careful study, changing attitudes and a good deal of comprehension are required to diminish the consequences of these often traumatic experiences. The Task Force on Toy Libraries for children and parents from different cultural backgrounds, established in the Netherlands, is a good example of an attempt to bring the nature of play opportunities into line with the cultural, socio-economic and geographic requirements of the individuals concerned.

However, in spite of these socio-cultural variations, a number of changes in the way people live have caused problems that are similar the world over. For instance, living in a highly congested urban area in Hong Kong is in terms of availability of space not all that different from living in Amsterdam or New York, Buenos Aires or New Delhi. All these conglomerates have one characteristic in common, namely a lack of spaces to play. Some of the following chapters deal with this issue and indicate a number of innovative programs to alleviate this situation.

The level of industrialization of a given society also has a strong influence on play, more particularly on the nature and intent of it. The western world, with its emphasis on efficiency, productivity and rationality, has by its nature a negative attitude towards play, as it is "not serious" and irrational. Therefore, play is often considered superfluous, frivolous and even dangerous for the production process. It is admitted, not for its intrinsic value, but as an opportunity to relax, to "recharge the battery" and to prepare oneself for the activity that really counts, namely work.

In the developing world, on the other hand, play often has a utilitarian purpose. As a number of the examples will show, play in those countries is often used as a form of non-formal education, teaching certain skills and preparing youngster for their role in life. However, one must be careful with generalizations. As the International Year of the Child Discussion Papers indicate, large and important variations characterize the developing world and it would be wrong to assume that in those societies play always occupies an important place on the value scale or that children always have sufficient space to play.

Some of the basic *concerns* relative to play and play opportunities for the child which will be addressed in the theme chapters include:

● The lack of opportunity to develop initiative and creativity. Living in an environment that is characterized by notions of consumerism and materialism often result in attitudes of expecting to be served, of passivity, and of superficiality. When all one has to do is buy a product without having to be involved in its creation, one can hardly be expected to develop a feeling of commitment, ownership and belonging. It is therefore important that children, somehow, be involved as participants in the decision-making processes relative to the matters that affect them.

• Another concern, and one we discussed above, is that of exploitation and importation of play situations that are alien to the child's culture. Cultures are dynamic and adaptable and, therefore, they change. However, this process of change is an evolutionary one and cannot be artificially accelerated.

• Children are frequently alienated socially; their play and learning opportunities are set aside and separated from the daily life of the community. As a consequence they frequently lack the important intergenerational contacts. This process of social alienation is further reinforced when both parents work or the child grows up in the rapidly increasing number of one-parent families. Added to this must be some of the consequences of urban living which has, for all intents and purposes, made the street inaccessible for the development of play experiences.

• Schools frequently over-emphasize formal academic studies at the expense of informal learning through play. This, plus the competition of the marketplace, fosters the development of highly competitive atmospheres in schools, frequently creating pressures and tensions for young people. This emphasis on academic studies, at the expense of educating people to prepare for and enjoy leisure, accentuates the development of the consumer attitude we talked about. In view of the growing availability of free time, it has become imperative that the educational system change its emphasis and include leisure-orientated teaching in the curricula, familiarizing students with a wide range of options and a positive attitude towards free time as a significant medium for growth and development.

United Nations   *D. Mangurian/United Nations*

• Space for play is often lacking or misused. One has only to look at the many schoolyards that are sterile and vacant for most of the time,

5

quite apart from the paucity of their condition. But not only the school yards are either not available or lack the proper provisions. Modern high-rises also stand out as examples having a total lack of play opportunities for children of all ages. At the other end of the spectrum, the thousands of children for whom shantytown is the only environment also lack the most basic of play opportunities.

• The prevailing attitude frequently still is that play is unimportant and peripheral. Consequently, urban planners with a proper appreciation for its significance are still extremely rare and legislation guaranteeing minimum provisions are virutally non-existent. Concomittant with this is the lowly status of play leaders, which is reflected in the frequently poor training-opportunities and low salaries.

• The last concern that we want to mention, and one that is really central to many others, is that of economic constraints. Play provision is not economically viable, and thus not an economic priority. Therefore, even in cases where the proper attitudes and conditions begin to develop, its existence remains precarious. Play opportunities belong within the social concerns and these are normally the first to fall victim to limitations in the availability of funds.

It is therefore imperative that those concerned with children and their opportunities to play continue their efforts to obtain the recognition play needs—the same priority as provisions for health, education and other social services.

Footnotes

1. Huizinga, Johan. *Homo Judens*, Boston, United States of America: Beacon Press, 1950, p.1.

2. *IPA Declaration for the Child's Right to Play*, International Association for the Child's Right to Play, Sheffield, England, 1977.

Some Issues and Consequences

T he main purpose for writing this book has been to provide a record of the ways in which countries of varying socio-cultural and economic backgrounds provide play opportunities for their children, how they integrate these into the living environment, and how, in sometimes significantly different ways, they all underline the close correlation that exists between playing, living and learning.

The underlying cause for the development of these programs has become increasingly universal. Modern means of communication and the rapid spread of the mass media are the main reasons why virtually all parts of the world, albeit in differing degrees, have come under the influence of modern methods of production, distribution and consumption. In consequence, all regions of the world are faced with the results of these phenomena. All must cope with the problems of urbanization, consumerism, competition, mass culture and alienation, and the problems associated with mass media, migration, bureaucratization and rationalization that seriously affect people's lifestyles. Leadership and authority are being questioned, values are changing and people's capacity to adapt is continuously challenged.

A discussion of the impact of these issues in the various regions of the world obviously falls far outside the scope of this book. It seems to us useful, however, to look at them from the point of view of their impact on play and the opportunity to play.

For instance, one of the consequences of industrialization is the creation of rapidly growing **urban areas.** Modern means of production, requiring the concentration of large numbers of workers at or near the place of work, continue to empty the rural areas and have a profound impact on the way children live. They no longer feel close to nature; animals, fields and forests are increasingly alien to them. The city, with its emphasis on efficiency, speed and impersonal relations, excludes them and has no time for them. Worst of all, it does not provide them with

Children's Environments Advisory Service

the space to play, experiment, explore and discover — all essential ingredients of a harmonious growing-up process.

The vacant lots have all but disappeared, traffic speed and density have made the streets inaccessible to playing children, and living in high-rise buildings deprives them of virtually all space.

The examples cited in the following chapters, and more in particular the one on Play Streets, are testimonies to the efforts concerned people have made to alleviate this situation, trying to create environments in which children can play and develop. Projects like the Woonerven in the Netherlands, the Spielstrassen in Germany, and the Environmental Yard in the United States of America are excellent examples of how even a modern metropolis can still provide adequate play opportunities. The "Adventure Playgrounds", "Children's Farms" and "Children's Gardens" are equally fascinating attempts to re-establish contact with animals and the natural environment.

One of the most complex and potentially most devastating effects of modern society is that of *consumerism.* Children growing up in a world of relative affluence, increasingly represented by its service industries, are encouraged to develop the attitude of consumers of products and buyers of privileges. This attitude prevents them from feeling a part of what they do, of developing a sense of ownership and of belonging. This is probably the most disturbing aspect of twentieth-century living, because it reduces participation to a shallow experience, inhibiting the exercise of creativity, inventiveness and originality.

Probably the most important mission of educators, parents and all those who are concerned is to change consumers into real participants, who have a commitment to what they are doing and who feel that they are part of it. They do not simply consume the product, but play an active part in its production.

This is not an easy task. People born into a society of affluence as children of parents who, for the most noble of reasons, are determined that their children will never be in want of anything, grow up expecting to be entertained without having to play a role other than that of a consumer or spectator. The tendency is reinforced by the fact that they are often alone. The same parents who provide their children with everything, frequently forget to give them of the most important commodity, a few moments of their own time.

More or less in line with this is concern about the nature of the products offered and questions about the potential harm war toys and other replicas of violent implements can have on a child's development. Questions such as those have still to be satisfactorily answered; subjective evidence however suggests that extreme care and vigilance is called for.

A large number of examples cited in the book are attempts to bring about changes of attitude and are developed for the purpose of developing in children their creative capacity, not only to satisfy their need to build, but also their need to be involved, to be and feel part of whatever they do and not to be just passive consumers. "Make-it-Yourself," "Kids Radio Van," "Jahrmarkt Spielbus", "Playcarts," and "Adventure Playgrounds", are excellent examples of these attempts to change consumers into active participants.

Another phenomenon that appears to have become increasingly prominent is that of *competition.* The advent of the industrial society has made competition one of the central aspects of life. One competes for markets, better means of production, jobs, results at school and, in a lot of cases, a simple "place in the sun". This emphasis on competition found a fertile soil in the world of play. Many games are based on the principle that a winner be declared: the team that scores the most goals, the athletes who jump farthest or run fastest, or the boat that outsails all others.

As competition became more ruthless in the production process and occupied an increasingly central place in daily living, its emphasis in the world of play became felt more distinctly, to the point where indeed it became "the only thing". The unfortunate side effect of this development has been that games of compeition no longer tolerate the weak, small or mediocre. Those who cannot "help the team" find no place in it, and those who lack the capacity to outperform the others are relegated to the side lines.

That this tendency leads to serious problems of confidence, security and self-esteem is clear. The stress and tensions that surround participation under these circumstances hamper the emotional and social development of those who have fallen victim to this "win at all cost" syndrome. The chapter on Games; New Ways to Play Them, gives an encouraging array of examples of attempts to break this cycle and bring back the emphasis on participation by all, cooperation, the development of social skills, the elements of joy and satisfaction.

The fact that the "New Games" of the United States of America and the "Cooperative Games" of Canada have, in the short time of their existence, spread over most parts of the world, is ample proof of a desire to turn away from the over emphasis on competition and winning and return to participation for participation's sake. It seems that through this process we are beginning to rediscover the values transmitted by the games of the Inuit of Canada's Northland, the Papuas of new Guinea and the Aboriginies of New Zealand.

Another issue that will have far reaching consequences for the world of tomorrow is that of *migration.* Prior to the Second World War, the demographic picture of most countries of the world remained reasonably stable. The available means of communication still restricted the movement of people, and lack of knowledge and cultural barriers often prevented settlement in faraway lands.

Since the late forties, however, initially as an emotional aftermath of the war and later as the result of political upheavals, economic instability, or problems connected with exponential population growth, the urge and necessity to relocate caused millions of people to pick up stakes, aided by greatly improved means of transportation and a growing familiarity with hitherto strange parts of the world.

Although this phenomenon has significantly influenced the size and composition of the population of countries like Canada, Australia and the United States of America, the changes have been relatively harmonious. Immigrants into these and other countries have been from cultural backgrounds similar to that of the resident population. This trend, however, is already changing and will drastically change in the near future. Western Europe knows the phenomenon of "gast arbeiders" or "fremd-arbeiter", workers "imported" to meet specific labour shortages, representing numbers that begin to make their imprint felt on the respective societies, especially with respect to the educational and other social systems.

Other countries have, as a result of de-colonization, seen their population grow with large numbers of former colonials, uprooted from a significantly different cultural background and introduced to an environment that shows serious problems of adapting to the influx. But, inevitably, the most profound influence on the demographic portrait of the world will be produced by a disproportionate population growth in various regions of the world. The fact that the industrialized countries are seeing their proportion of yound people diminish while that of those in their sixties and over increases (whereas in most of the third world countries the opposite happens), has created a situation in which western countries are "greying", whereas third world ones are characterized by the youth of their people. In absolute numbers, too, the third world countries continue to show accelerated population increases, while the industrialized ones exhibit a tendency to slow down or even produce a negative rate of growth. When one furthermore considers that the growth in employment opportunities in third world countries is not expected to absorb the increasing number of workers, the conclusion is inevitable that large numbers will go and seek their fortunes elsewhere.

A beginning of this phenomenon is already noticeable in a number of the southern states of the United States of America, where, as a result of this, de facto bilingualism, English and Spanish, is in effect. This migrationary pattern will, in our opinion, become a universal phenomenon, placing high demands on the adaptive qualities of recipient populations and settlers alike.

One of the crucial areas of this meeting of cultures will be the schools, and the most effective realm to arrive at a smooth adaptation will be that of play. It is therefore of special significance that all those involved with children be aware of this phenomenon, realize its potential for enriching experiences, have an open ear and mind for the inevitable cultural conflicts that will arise, but be determined to assist the children to develop mutually beneficial attitudes.

That the world of play will undergo strong influences in this process is clear; traditional patterns will be modified and new ones introduced. The place of the child in the receiving culture may be influenced. The western world, having developed into an alien one for children, "sets aside" spaces to play, allowing its children in only on special occasions and under special conditions, "seen but not heard". In many other cultures, children are an integral part of society; their presence is everywhere. A play space need not be "set aside" because the entire neighbourhood is shared with the children. An interesting observation was made in an article describing Dutch mothers visiting a play area together with Moroccan mothers. The author tells us that the Dutch mothers knitted while their children played, whereas the Moroccan mothers played with their children.

Although migration is a recent phenomenon and therefore the number of intercultural projects limited, we did receive some, for instance "Migrant Child Development Program" and "Inter-Action Games Method".

An issue of special importance is that of *equal opportunity*, which goes far beyond the simple question of admittance. Problems of economics, the acquisition of skills, language difficulties, and a host of social taboos, often prevent real involvement on the part of new arrivals. Social taboos especially are frequently real barriers to integration, and the removal of these ought to be of prime concern.

A population group for which the question of equal opportunity is of particular significance is that of the handicapped. The International Year of the Disabled Persons, proclaimed for 1981, has moved this question a little more to the centre of our attention. The discussion around integration and segregation has intensified, and the call for special provisions in buildings and other facilities to allow access by the handicapped obtained a universal quality.

We have felt that a detailed discussion of these issues falls outside the scope of this book. Although philosophically in favour of the movement toward integration of disabled children into the overall play opportunities, we realize that certain situations and specific conditions make the development of segregated programs desirable. The examples we have discussed reflect both points of view.

For instance, whereas most of the "Adventure Playgrounds", "Children's Farms," and "City Farm" projects stress integration, the "Let's-Play-To-Grow" program is directed almost exclusively to children with special needs.

A social institution receiving growing attention, and which is increasingly seen as central to the solution of most of the issues and problems we have identified, is that of the *family.* It is virtually impossible, in the context of a chapter that addresses itself to a wide cultural spectrum, to make specific observations on the place and role of the family in modern society.

However, a few general observations seem warranted. First of all, it can be said that the concept of the family has undergone changes. The extended family, once the universal model, consisting of a wide range of persons united by reasons of blood relationship, has in most countries, especially industrialized ones, been replaced by the nuclear family, typically consisting of father, mother and one or two children.

But not only composition and size have changed. The role of the nuclear family is no longer that of its extended forerunner: education has increasingly been taken over by the educational system, care for old and sick relatives has become the task of the social institutions, and recreational agencies have taken over most of the concern for free-time provisions for the family members. Furthermore, television, radio and other media compete with the conveyors of traditional values in the struggle for priority. Consequently, the central role the extended family had is now increasingly shared between the nuclear one and a host of government and private agencies.

To this picture must be added the phenomenon of the extension of the family concept to include not only those united by relationship of blood, but all those with whom one can feel in communion, either as members of the same household, a combination of households, or without any territorial connections. Thus we have seen the advent of the one-parent family, the reconstituted family, the fusioned family, communes, homosexual households and many more.

That the place of and responsibility for the child has become increasingly unspecific and vague in this conglomerate of models goes without saying. We have already seen that much of the tasks that fell to the family have, in time, been taken over by school, playgrounds, social services, campsites, recreational centres and other agencies among which, with the recent phenomenon of the working mother, daycare centres have acquired special importance.

That this proliferation of involvements threatens to diffuse the focus of responsibility is clear. It is therefore understandable that, in all parts of the world, initiatives are developed for the purpose of narrowing the perspective and of attempting to more clearly identify where, and with which institution, the main responsibility for the provision of play opportunities lies.

Other than this jurisdictional concern there is another one that deals with attempts to provide a greater feeling of purpose, direction, stability and security to children in a world that has become increasingly pluralistic. Pluralistic in the sense of being composed of a growing number of autonomous institutions which, having developed their own norms and values, demand allegiance to these values for the time the child falls under their respective jurisdictions. For instance, certain values are stressed within the family, but these are not necessarily identical to those professed by the youth organizations or the school or the peer group or the work environment. The results is that it has become increasingly difficult for children to develop a clear idea as to who they are and where they are at. In other words, our pluralistic world threatens to develop pluralistic identities.

In days gone by, the situation was entirely different. All social institutions reflected one set of values, namely those of the church. One could move from one to the other feeling at home, because what was considered the norm in the one corresponded with that which prevailed in the other. Identities were built harmoniously as one moved along.

These concerns have caused people in various parts of the world, but primarily in the highly industrialized countries, to feel that probably the family unit might be able to play the unifying value role that used to be played by the church. They believe that the family should and could become the stabilizing factor that has been lost, because it has the potential to provide its children with a clear sense of identity, direction and purpose.

On the basis of these considerations, a growing number of family programs have been developed around the world. We have reported on the "Time Out" program in Australia, the "Familien Spiel" in Germany, the "Famly Recreation Program" in New Zealand, the "Pedagogical Play Centre" in Norway, the "Let's-Play-to-Grow" program in the United States of America and the "Family Camp for Pre-Schoolers" in Uruguay.

In most of these projects, the family concept is taken in the enlarged sense, including not only the nuclear family but also single parents, grandparents, aunts, uncles and friends, creating a unit that can become the focal point for the development of the child through the medium of play. This unit can provide a sense of stability and belonging, in a world where so much seems to be drifting without sense of direction or purpose.

Robin Moore

Children's Participation

The purpose of this chapter is to discuss the participation of children in all aspects of play opportunities. Frequently, when we think of children as participants we limit this to the consumer phase of the overall process. Normally we do not see their involvement beyond that of players of games or as users of facilities; in other words, as the beneficiaries of opportunities others, primarily adults, have developed for them.

"Planning with the child in mind" often serves as the ultimate indication of our concern for the needs, desires and aspirations of the clients, who can only hope that what is "in the mind" corresponds reasonably well with their real needs, desires and aspirations. Our contention is that those for whom a given opportunity is meant, in this case children, must not only participate in the implementation phase of it, but must also play a central role in its planning and evaluation. We furthermore want to stress the significant contribution children can make as teachers and leaders of other children. Based on these considerations, we will in this chapter deal with the following aspects:

- children's participation in planning and evaluation;
- their involvement in the implementation and developmental phase;
- children as teachers and change agents.

But first a few general observations. Participation is a much maligned concept, more often than not, used to cover various forms of manipulation. It is used to give citizens the right to express opinions on matters affecting them; advisory councils and consultative bodies are created under its guise. However, unless those thus consulted are given a share in the power structure, these forms of participation will remain meaningless. The essence of participation is the delegation of power, the power to share in the decision-making process relative to the planning and evaluation of a project, but also to share the power required for its implementation. This means that participation needs to go much further than the right to express one's opinion. Whether this is done by means of public meetings or advisory bodies, is relatively insignificant, and in many cases meaningless, unless those whose opinion is sought share in the ultimate responsibility for the overall program.

The often heard objection that this procedure "takes too long", "never leads to concrete results", and that "the most effective committee is the one-man committee", is based on an inappropriate appreciation of the real merits of the participatory process and needs to be most energetically opposed. Those who have been involved in these processes know that the participatory route is indeed a long and often circuitous one. However, they also know that time thus spent in the beginning is easily gained at the end, because the program that emerges is a true reflection of the wishes, desires and aspirations of the various constituencies and has therefore the best chances of achieving its stated objectives.

In recent years, the principle of involving those for whom a given program is developed, in all its phases, is achieving increasing recognition and is being applied more and more, re-establishing as it were processes that were quite commonly adopted in pre-industrial days. The industrial society, with its highly sophisticated system of specializations (a consequence of technological development), introduced an era where the planning process was also relegated to the domain of the specialist.

The renewed emphasis on the participatory process, however, is almost entirely limited to adults. When we deal with children, their participation in the planning process is considered farfetched and unworkable. The main reason for this attitude is that we still think in stereotypes: planning means committees, meetings, boardrooms and, therefore, procedure and formality, two notions that are far removed from the world of a 10- or 12- year old child. Therefore, if we want to involve children in the process, we will have to change the traditional planning models, introducing changes that will create the opportunity for real and meaningful participation.

How can this be brought about? Planning has, over time, developed into a sophisticated area of specialization, consisting of a series of logically designed steps that lead to a specified end. Introducing into this sequence effective mechanisms for participation by children seems like an almost impossible mission.

It is obvious that not all ages can share in the decision-making process to the same degree. Children's ability to participate varies with their physical, social and intellectual development. Furthermore, childhood is culturally determined; the assignment of responsibility to children varies with the place they occupy in the social fabric of a given culture. They are called upon to play different roles in different societies and these will invariably be reflected in the degree and manner of their ability to participate in the planning process.

As will be demonstrated by an example later on in this chapter, the attitude of the adults is extremely important in this regard. As was stated in the *Childhood City Newsletter*, December, 1980, "The degree of opportunity for a child of any age to collaborate with adults in the every day management of family, community, and all of the institutions they attend, is directly reflected in the competence and sense of responsibility held by adults in the society."[1]

Although a number of projects have been developed aimed at studying ways and means of obtaining children's active participation, we are still far from having workable solutions.

Various studies have shown that children have a rather clear idea of what they want and how they would like to see their environment changed. One of these was developed for the Norwegian Institute of Urban and Regional Research.[2] The study dealt with problems connected with planning in one of the older parts of the city of Oslo. In the course of meetings and discussions with the people concerned, it became clear that one of the crucial issues was the lack of safe and stimulating areas where children could play. Based on this fact, the researchers decided to let the children speak for themselves and tell the planners how they perceived their neighbourhood and how they would want to change it.

The method applied varied from the traditional questionnaire-type survey. Half the 7- to 12-year olds were asked to make drawings of their journey to school and answer a few questions; the other half would write about their opportunities to play. A total of 123 descriptive answers and 183 drawings were received. As was to be expected, the younger children preferred to draw, whereas the older ones showed a preference for written stories.

Analysis of the essays showed that:
– 31 per cent wished there were fewer cars;
– 45 per cent missed or wanted more, larger and better equipped playgrounds;
– 17 per cent wanted meadows, large fields or parks that could be used for a variety of activities;
– 19 per cent wanted places for specific athletic activties, such as swimming, cycling, skating, skiing and soccer.

The drawings showed that there should be more playgrounds. While only 13 per cent had playgrounds in their drawings of today's situation, 42 per cent had drawn playgrounds and soccer fields in their pictures of the desired environment.

The drawings furthermore showed that children want small houses. On the drawings of the future, houses did not dominate the street; they had fewer floors than those depicting today's situation. When cars disappear and the houses are small, more space is given to children, a fact that shows up clearly in the drawings.

A desire for greener and more pleasant neighbourhoods emerges from both the drawings and the essays. Thirty-four per cent wrote that they wanted grass, flowers and trees in backyards and where they play.

The study showed quite a discrepancy between the present reality and that which the children would like to see. The project clearly underlined the necessity of basing the planning of facilities and programs for children on the perceptions they have of their needs and desires. It shows that it is wrong to take for granted that children, especially the very young, lack the facility to express these aspirations and that therefore adults and, in most cases, parents must act as their interpreters. The children participating in this study showed a surprising capacity to articulate their wants and feelings; they only needed to be given the opportunity.

This study and many others of this nature, important as they may be, do not go beyond expressing the views and opinions children have of issues that immediately affect them. They do not solve the problem of how to facilitate their active participation in the planning process.

An attempt to have this take place was initiated by the Stichting Ruimte in the Netherlands. The project was developed in Rotterdam in 1979, for the purpose of studying ways and means of involving children in the planning process for an urban renewal project.[3] Other objectives included stimulation of cooperation between the educational and sociocultural agencies, experimentation with working on a real project, and changing the attitudes concerning the place of children in the Dutch society. Participants included children between 11 and 14-years old, of the 6th grade of an elementary school, one teacher, one socio-cultural worker and one student of social work.

The project headquarters were an elementary school and a neighbourhood clubhouse. In the school part of the project, the children collected information on a number of subjects, such as urban renewal, traffic patterns, play spaces, etc. They discussed the information obtained, studied films, asked questions, looked at photographs and wrote papers on the subjects. In the clubhouse section they formed an action group which took the results of the school part of the project and, based on these, developed a proposal for the creation of a playstreet. The method used was that of role playing — the children represented the mayor, aldermen, residents, police, journalists and children. They presented the results to the alderman responsible for urban renewal, complete with drawings, photos, traffic reports and other pertinent data. Following this, there was a public meeting at which the children explained their views and proposals, illustrated with slides and an exhibition.

Although a complete evaluation of the project is, at this time, not available, a few observations can already be made

As we said in the beginning, the traditional planning model, including meetings and allocation of tasks, poses difficulties. The logic of initiating action, holding meetings, etc. does not harmonize with the logic of children's activities. They feel much more comfortable with concrete tasks.

Children do not represent a coherent group. There are individual and group differences, especially in the Dutch example where the participants included children from foreign workers and overseas parts of the country. These differences strongly influence the group dynamic process; furthermore, the things they find especially important differ between boys and girls, middle-class and lower-class families.

The project did not succeed in establishing real contact with the neighbourhood; it took place in typical "child-places" in which the children were segregated from the outside world (school and clubhouse). Therefore, although a project of this nature may have to start in a segregated setting, it must, as soon as feasible, be integrated into the overall planning structures. Otherwise the danger exists that a method such as the one that was developed creates, in a subtle way, a new form of segregation.

The problem of having children recognized as residents and participants is still formidable. Organizing the children, and connecting them with, in the case of the Dutch study, the urban-renewal process, meets not only structural and procedural difficulties, but also attitudinal barriers on the part of adults.

A preliminary conclusion to be drawn from this example appears to be that, before embarking upon a children's participation project, the overall situation must be studied carefully. Questions related to the realistic chances of such a project, attitudes towards children, the political situation, organization of the planning, design and management and many more need to be looked into carefully.

A few international and national organizations are becoming more vocal in advocating involvement of children and youth in planning processes. For instance, the International Youth Federation for Environmental Studies and Conservation, sponsored by the International Union for the Conservation of Nature and Natural Resources, located in Strassbourg, France, is involved in the promotion of participation by young people in environmental projects.

The International Association for the Child's Right to Play supports children's participation by promoting concepts like the Adventure Playgrounds where children have direct control over the shaping of their immediate environment. The International Union for Child Welfare, through its project *For Every Child a Tree*, has successfully involved children in a number of re-forestation projects in Africa, and the International Cooperative Alliance, with its emphasis on cooperative education, includes youth as active participants in many of its third world projects.

National organizations stressing children's participation include the United States of America's *Architects in Schools* program funded by the National Endowment for the Arts, and the Belgian *Met Open Oog Op Weg*, supported by the Koning Boudewyn Stichting, Brussels. The American program has the potential of developing into a participatory one although, at the present time, the involvement of young people is only marginal. Projects include classroom improvement and improvement of the school environment as a whole.

The Belgian program is explicitly meant to involve children in improving their environment with the assistance of teachers and youth workers as "animateurs". We discussed this in some detail in the chapter "Play: A Social and Educational Medium".

Another national program, interesting because of the active involvement of the commercial sector, is the **Better Britain Competition**, sponsored by Shell U.K. Its objectives are similar to those of *Met Open Oog Op Weg* (Walking Around With Your Eyes Open).

All these examples show a rapidly growing awareness of the need to involve children, somehow or other, in the planning process of projects that affect them. The difficulty still lies in that "somehow or other". In spite of the encouraging number of projects attempting to find ways and means, we have yet to come up with a satisfactory model. It is certain that the traditional planning models are unworkable and that probably entirely new approaches will have to be developed with the children concerned. It is equally clear that, in order to bring this about, significant changes have to occur in the attitudes of adults involved in the planning process. It seems to us that probably the attitudinal barriers will prove to be the most difficult to overcome and the most essential to remove.

Participation by children in the evaluation of projects is much easier to bring about and much more common. Counsellors in a summer camp, for instance, will frequently talk to their charges to find out whether or not they like a certain activity, or what they would have preferred instead; and leaders of an aquatic program will want to know what their pupils particularly liked or disliked. The reason for this greater involvement in the evaluation phase of a project lies in the nature of the process. Whereas planning is an integrated process from the very beginning, evaluation initially takes place along two parallel lines, staff and participants each evaluating the program separately.[4] This part of the evaluation process therefore is quite universally implemented. The problem arises with the subsequent phases during which staff and participants must come together to identify possible divergent results, if needed, establish new criteria and modify the program. These phases obviously pose the same problem as those discussed for the planning process and therefore, here too, radically new approaches, resulting in the development of new models will have to be designed.

Examples of children's involvement in the implementation phase of programs are fortunately much more common. The activity leader who proceeds according to firmly laid-down and adhered-to procedures is becoming increasingly rare. All over the world, we notice a growing awareness that children are quite capable of articulating their desires and of expressing them in appropriate alterations of objectives as well as operating procedures of games.

The theme chapters of this book provide ample testimony of this fact. An example of this and one that is particularly interesting because of its somewhat unusual subject matter and physical setting is the one developed by the Open University in Oxford, England.

The project is called *Children and Video* and its purposes were to show that television can be used creatively by nearly anyone, that play is essential in the process of creating, and that children, even very young ones, are capable of using television to create and express ideas to others.

The participants were children between the ages of five and seven, using portable video equipment. Initially, they were left completely free to determine how they wanted to use the video, which was not an easy principle to follow for the leaders. As most adults, they found it difficult to see the value of play when there is no apparent result. Another problem was that the children were often more interested in doing than in communicating their experiences. Gradually more structure was introduced, helping the children not only to use the camera with greater ease, but also assisting them to focus more clearly on a definite form for their experience. They began to create plays and acquired experience with shooting in different environments.

The third aspect of children's participation we wanted to discuss is that of the child as teacher. A number of programs come to mind in this respect. For instance, there is the *Help a Kid* project, developed by the Boys' Clubs of America, which is intended to encourage teenagers to learn about, and become involved with younger children in the Boys' club and throughout their community.

A similar program has for years been successfully operated by the YMCA's *Leaders Clubs*, which provide valuable leadership experiences to boys and girls from nine years of age and up. These clubs have, over the many years of their existence, proven to be extremely successful from the point of view of the programs offered by the Y's. But, more importantly, they have also been successful because of their influence on the lives of large numbers of boys and girls who, through the clubs and thanks to the service opportunities they offered, have been able to grow and develop in a way they could never have acquired otherwise.

The clubs operate in a variety of ways depending on the respective local situations. However, they all have in common a basic structure which exists of two parts. First there is a theoretical part during which the young people receive instructions in basic leadership techniques and the skills required for their area of interests. Second, there is a service part during which the leader is required to perform a minimum number of hours of voluntary service as a leader of a given activity group.

And finally we want, in this context, to draw attention to the *CHILD to Child* program that was conceived and established by the Institute of Child Health and the Institute of Education, both of the University of London, England. The occasion was the International Year of the Child and the program was designed primarily for the Third World, in particular for the poorer communities of its more remote rural areas, inner city, and shanty-town settlements. It teaches and encourages children of school-age to concern themselves with the health and general development of their younger brothers and sisters, and of other younger children in their community.

Simple preventive and curative activities, as well as games, and role playing are taught to the children in school as well as youth groups and through other channels, so that they may pass ideas on in the family or community environment.

The tradition of older children being responsible, during non-school hours, for their younger siblings is well established in all of the lesser developed countries; the poorer the community, the more common the practice and the earlier the age at which children accept this responsibility.

The range of activities to be undertaken in the program is limitless. For the purpose of our investigation it is of interest to note that "Toys and Games" and "Playing with Younger Children" figure among the most popular. A special point of concern in these approaches is the child who has never attended school which, among girls in some parts of the world, amounts to 80 percent of the population.

A considerable number of programs have been developed in a large number of countries around the world. These include Chile, Guatemala, Kuwait, New Guinea, Morroco, Sudan, Tanzania and many more.

As a closing example we want to discuss a project that may well become a model for the role children can play in the shaping of a participatory society. It is called '***Gruppo Futuro***', Community Participation by Children in Futures.[5.] The originators of the project, who belong to the Open University Oxford Research Unit, England, wanted to create a process permitting children to experiment actively with as many media as possible in order to express, propose, question and build alternate futures with minimal interference from adults.

The project involves two state schools in Naples, Italy — one in a middle-class area and one in a newly constructed poor district — and two in Oxford, England — one in a multi-social, mixed first-language and mixed income area, and the other an educational sub-normal school in a predominantly working-class area. The Italian schools are integrated in the sense that handicapped children take part in everyday school life.

The initial idea, and the one that became the basis for the entire project, was that change and different futures are possible; the role of the "animateurs" consisted mainly in creating an environment where change was acceptable and in providing a wide array of communication tools to the children.

The project provided the children with great freedom compared to that normally offered by the schools; greater freedom to ask questions, research, experiment and to play and mix activities of body and mind which hitherto had been separated. The children developed their own words and images, standards and aesthetics. The children's free access to media broke the artificial barriers of classroom and timetabling and carried the futures out to the community. Children organized debates and exhibitions; they often used the corridors of the school as experimental areas by posting placards and questions; they decided when to go outside the school to research and discuss ideas (using tape recorders for example) with people in the community. In most instances there were conflicts with the school structure. The conflicts were positive in that the nature of schooling and the opposing philosophy of the futures project were openly confronted with children as protagonists in the discussions. For example, children refused to take part in a conference exhibit organized by the Naples city Administration after they discovered that they could neither participate in the conference planning nor decide the layout of their work.

A very interesting observation made by the project leaders was that, throughout the duration of the Gruppo Futuro and the work of a parallel group in northern Italy entitled "Little Mount Olympus Co-operative", films, slide-tapes, video-tapes, poems, etc. made by sub-normal or difficult children revealed the same creative change as those made by normal children. These projects appear to destroy myths concerning the capacities of privileged or disadvantaged children. Most futures projects with children tend to select gifted children as participants (seen as potential leaders; only these children are allowed to propose alternatives). This practice, according to the author of the project, like the segregation of sub-normal children into special schools, is the antithesis of participation in futures, which they feel should be continuous, integrated into real life situations and inclusive of everyone, not just an elite.

The experience with Gruppo Futuro has shown that children's ideas and images of futures are radically different from those of adults. Many of the thoughts expressed are probably unrealizable. Nevertheless, the extension of futures participation in space and time implies a great change in adults' perception of children. Children can become cultural innovators, change agents and protagonists in a society in which their voices, words and images are as valid as those of adults. Learning and cultural flow are no longer one-way from adult to child but instead are multi-directional; the young can teach the middle-aged, the very old, the very young, and so forth in infinite directions and combinations.

The outward nature of children's participation in futures may well indicate the slow dissolution of the school as the fundamental centre for learning and information, and its replacement by the community. Learning thus becomes integrated with living and theory with practice.

Footnotes

1. "What is Participation" in *Childhood City Newsletter*, New York, N.Y., No. 22, 1980, p. 7.

2. Kolbenstvedt, Marika. *"The children of Toyon describe their district: The use of children's compositions and drawings as a research method"*, paper presented to International Federation of Pedestrian Association, Norway, 1976, pp. 13–15.

3. Willem de Zeeuw, Jan et al. *Young Peoples Participation in Planning, Design and Management of their Surroundings in Rotterdam*, Stichting Ruimte, Rotterdam, Netherlands, 1979, pp. 3–8.

4. For further information on evaluation see Banon, Joseph. *Leisure Resources: Its Comprehensive Planning*, New Jersey, U.S.A.: Prentice-Hall Inc., 1976, Chapter 6.

5. Information taken from *The Political Implications of Child Participation: Steps Toward a Participatory Democracy*, a paper by Simon Nicholson and Raymond Lorenzo, Gruppo Futuro, Open University, Oxford Research Team, Oxford, England and Napoli, Italy, 1979, pp. 3–8.

Reference materials used in the preparation of this chapter include:

Childhood City Newsletters, The Centre for Human Environment, New York, N.Y., U.S.A., No. 22, 1980, No. 23, 1981.

Kolbenstvedt, Marika. *The children of Toyon describe their district: The use of children's compositions and drawings as a research method*, paper presented to International Federation of Pedestrian Association, Norway, 1976.

Willem de Zeeuw, Jan et al. *Young Peoples Participation in Planning, Design and Management of their surroundings in Rotterdam*, Stichting Ruimte, Rotterdam, Netherlands, 1979.

Dunn, Katherine. *Children and Video: 'camera one, I'm filming you'*, The Open University, Oxford, England, 1976.

Help a Kid, Boys' Clubs of America, New York, N.Y., U.S.A., 1975.

Aarons, Audrey and Hugh Hawes, *Child-to-Child*, London, England: Macmillan Press Ltd., 1979.

Nicholson, Simon and Raymond Lorenzo. *The Political Implications of Child Participation: Steps Toward a Participatory Democracy*, Open University, Oxford, England, 1979.

Animals, Farms and Nature

I n this chapter we have brought together programs dealing with Animals, Children and
Youth Farms, and a variety of Environmental
programs. They all have in common an attempt to re-establish contact
between children and nature, and to help them develop healthy relationships with their natural environment through association with trees,
shrubs, vegetables, flowers, insects and animals.

Unfortunately, living in an increasingly urbanised environment is
progressively depriving children all over the world from the rich and
diverse sources of play materials and experiences nature can offer. For
many twentieth-century children, nature is an alien concept, and the
natural environment an unknown phenomenon.

It has therefore become necessary to, more or less artificially, create
conditions under which children have the opportunity to relate to animals, not as in a zoo, but to accept responsibility for them, to care for
them and learn to be at ease with them, to learn the wonders of growing
plants from seeds, and to acquire an appreciation for the important role
farms play in our lives.

Children and Youth Farms

Although all projects in this category use the word farm in their title,
most bear little resemblance to a real farm. With the exception of one type
of children's farm in the Netherlands, which has an educational focus and
where therefore children go to see a real farm in operation, the purpose of
the others differs in a number of respects. For instance, most are not
production oriented and a good number have rather drastically changed
their method of operation to accommodate the various educational purposes of the organizers.

Since a children and youth farm is not a farm in the traditional sense,
it may be useful to describe what type of establishment generally is

Kinderboerdij – *Stichting Recreatie*

Robin Moore

considered under that heading.

Based on the definition developed by the Netherlands Commission on Children's Farms of the Institute for Environmental Education one could say that a children's farm is a facility consisting of one or more farmlike buildings surrounded by fields accessible to visitors, the purpose of which is to establish contacts between man, nature and culture through the medium of experience, thus contributing to the development of nature and environmental awareness.

Children's farms operate under specific management, which means:

- the visitors get the opportunity to be actively involved in the management of the farm;
- the children's farm offers the opportunity to obtain information about animals and, if necessary, plants, nature or environment;
- the design and function of the children's farm are in tune with the character and needs of the residential area where the farm is situated;
- the activities can be organized for the purpose of creating interest in and understanding of nature, culture and environment in the broadest sense;
- in principle, only those animals that offer opportunity for direct contact and care should be part of the herd of a children's farm.

From this statement flow a number of general principles governing the operation of a children's farm, which can be formulated as follows:

Speelboerderij Elsenhove – *Hans Schippers*

- The number and kinds of staff required varies greatly with the size of the farm, the activities provided, the number and quality of volunteer help, available resources, and the farm's operating principles. Love for animals, patience and understanding of children, specific knowledge and experience are, in order of priority, considered the major characteristics of the successful supervisor.

• The farms are financed in a variety of ways. Most cover at least part of their expenses through participant's fees; some rent facilities to visiting school groups or private clubs; others grow their own feed and a number are subsidized by social clubs or voluntary agencies.

But virtually all become increasingly dependent on government support, which, in most cases, is the municipal government. For instance, the Children's Farms in the Netherlands are almost fully operated by local government and the City of Stuttgart in West Germany pays the salaries of the full time staff as well as fifty percent of the operating costs of the city's seventeen Youth Farms.

An important aspect of the children's involvement is the care for domesticated animals who can no longer fend for themselves. The children must be given the opportunity to feed them, in spite of the obvious risks involved. Clear instructions, a nucleus of permanent helpers, and regular check-ups by a veterinarian, will bring these down to acceptable levels. The farm should also have a rest-field where the animals can recover from too much feeding or too much attention.

Parents are frequently overly concerned for the transmittance of diseases by the animals. Obviously, the farm can never provide complete protection; attempts to reach that condition would render the entire experience meaningless. Reasonable precautions might include quarantine for new acquisitions, regular cleaning of stalls and stables, veterinary inspections and washing of hands after animal grooming.

Quite a few children are timid in the proximity of animals and some are outright frightened. Therefore, it is important that contact with the animals be structured in such a way that the children are exposed to the smaller animals first and, upon familiarization, gradually move to the larger specimens. For this purpose, it is preferable to use domesticated native animals and to select especially those breeds which have a high tolerance for contact with children. Although the addition of exotic animals may be very attractive, they harbour the danger of changing the farm into a "place to look and not to touch".

To illustrate the various approaches to Children and Youth farms, examples from Belgium, Canada, England, the Federal Republic of Germany, the Netherlands and Sweden will be discussed.

Belgium

The first *Children's Farms* in Belgium appeared in 1970 and have primarily developed in the Flemish part of the country. Although their objectives and organizational structures vary, they all share a desire to help reduce the estrangement from the natural processes which urbanization imposes.

The Belgian Children's Farms have three distinct objectives: a social one, an educational one and a recreational one. Based on those objectives, the following models have been developed:

• The *ferme-vitrine*, "show farms". This is the least interesting model; all the children can do is parade past the animals; intimate contact is impossible; the farm looks more like a zoo.

• A *day on the farm*. Some farms receive the children for a day; this format allows a certain participation in the life of the farm and a more immediate contact with the animals. Still, if the children come after school hours, they do miss a good deal of the farm activities which start much earlier.

• A *week on the farm*. Farms that are equipped to receive school classes for an entire week make it possible for the students to discover the work rhythm on the farm and to actually participate. It gives them the opportunity to use that which they have experienced immediately, because classes continue during their stay on the farm. Another advantage is that this way, they establish interpersonal relations in a different context.

• *The neighbourhood farm*. This type of farm is open the whole day. The children run it in part; they go there before or after school and during their holidays. Only when they go to the farm regularly can children discover nature's cycles. They are involved in the management and in the search for markets for the products. The farm is open to all members of the community: senior citizens have their gardens; each age group has its activities and its role. In this manner, the children discover mutual assistance relationships between the different generations.

This model is only possible if the farm is located in an urban context. Its success depends on the number of "animateurs". It has the advantage of bringing the children into touch with all aspects related to the operation of a farm, of accepting responsibility and of learning to understand the processes of production and reproduction.

Canada

The example from Canada represents a different category of projects which, however, have comparable objectives. This category deals with zoos and, more specifically, the modern zoos where traditional educational purposes, based on the "look and not touch" principle have, wherever possible, been replaced by a much more relaxed, play oriented atmosphere.

Such a zoo is the *Riverview Park and Zoo* in Peterborough, Ontario which, indeed, is not a zoo in the traditional sense. The emphasis is on freedom; freedom to wander through shaded parklands, to touch and feed domesticated animals, to enjoy floral displays, to play in the play-grounds, to barbeque in the field or simply to relax. This freedom includes that of access, for there is no charge for admission.

The entire development, which has its origin in a small zoo, started some 40 years ago, is based on visits by entire family groups and has grown into an enterprise containing well over 200 animals and birds, playgrounds, totem poles, barns, displays and a miniature railroad, all spread out over a 50-acre park.

England

Extremely interesting and imaginative applications of the farms and animals principle are the *City Farms*, developed by Inter-Action Trust, London. These involve animals and gardening on small plots of land in towns and cities. The land on which the project is built is normally land that is unused, such as deserted rights of way, old railroad beds, and, in one case, even an old cemetery.

The range of possibilities of a City Farm is unlimited; they can include riding stables and pets' corners, allotment gardens for the elderly, nature trails, bicycle tracks and open-air theatres. One of the main rationales for the development of City Farms, other than the need for children and adults to re-establish contact with nature, is the consideration that, in the future, money will probably no longer be available for the building of recreation centres, youth centres and community halls. Improvisation, self-help, and use of that which is available will therefore become the basis for the development of services.

City Farms can provide a viable alternative because they make a positive use of waste land; they require little capital lay-out; the sheds, paddocks, fences, etc. that are needed form an unattractive target for vandals, while at the same time creating a farm-like appearance, and they can be largely self-supporting.

The unique aspect of the City Farms is that they were started, not by planners, educators or technologists, but by non-specialists – the average man in the street.

Over thirty voluntary groups operate City Farms at the present time. They are set up on a business-like basis – every management group of users negotiates a proper lease or licence with the land owner and is formally incorporated. The activities are extremely varied and include gardening for senior citizens, for people from the neighbourhood, and for children, visits by school classes, picnics, drama and music activities, arts and crafts classes, riding lessons, plus a host of other things including such activities as car repairs and community projects. Most are operated on an integrated basis although a number of special classes for handicapped children are organized.

Finances are always a difficult issue; most farms are financed through earnings, donations and gifts in kind. The former can become an important source: riding lessons, use of facilities by schools, youth clubs or neighbourhood groups, the organization of social events and others. However, their chances of becoming self-sufficient are extremely small and most become increasingly dependent on government grants.

An example of a City Farm is the one at Cardiff, Wales, situated on four acres of wasteland, on the edge of two large urban communities, Grangetown and Riverside. The farm is but a short walk from the city centre and is overlooked by the wooded slopes of Leckwith Hill. The site has a 10-year lease from Cardiff City Council.

City Farms – *Inter-Action Trust*

It is unique in urban Wales. Its activities include landscaping of the site by local volunteers, working on the main buildings (farm house, study centre, animal barns, etc.), gardening by local groups and schools, and animal husbandry (bees, rabbits, poultry). Further projects include the addition of residential and loaned livestock (goats, pigs, sheep, ducks and geese) and small-scale carp farming.

The focal point of the farm, once completed, will be the study centre with meeting facilities, library and exhibition space for affiliated groups (gardeners, schools, etc.) and farm members. Training centres will be run with local agricultural and horticultural colleges and other associated groups, for instance community arts and crafts, weavers and beekeepers. Special projects and facilities are planned for the handicapped. There is a nominal charge for non-members, and refreshments are available in the farmhouse kitchen.

The farm opened in September 1979 and came about with initial funding from the Urban Aid Program, the Manpower Services Commission, the Prince of Wales Trust, and local charities. Numerous local firms have donated materials.

The City Farm movement publishes the "City Farm News", a comprehensive bi-monthly, written by City Farm groups and associated, and put together by Inter-Action's *City Farm Advisory Service*.

The Federal Republic of Germany

Probably the most comprehensive approach to meeting the children's needs to play, to develop practical skills, to learn to work together in groups, to build, to garden, to play with and look after animals, and to meet challenges is represented in the *Youth Farms*, developed under the auspices of the *Bund der Jugendfarmen und Aktivspielplätze EV*.

This organization assists with the development, in or near densely populated urban areas, of Youth Farms. Adventure Playgrounds are often incorporated into the farms. The result is an impressive series of developments across the country, combining the positive aspects of both. This approach provides the opportunity to build huts, lay fires, play music as well as look after animals, to garden and to take part in a whole host of

Adventure Playground at Jugendfarm   Jugendfarm – *Bund der Jugendfarmem und Aktivspielplätze*
Haldenweise – *Jane Knight*

social activities. The importance of this approach is that it stimulates the development of the whole child, its creative, physical, cognitive, as well as emotional faculties.

One of the more successful examples of this comprehensive approach is the *Jugendfarm Haldenwiese* close to Stuttgart.

As the diagram indicates, this playground combines all facilities one should expect to find in a children's and youth farm, with a village the children built, a place where one can make a fire, allotment gardens and a separate playground for the smaller children.

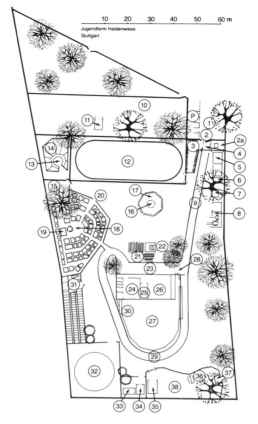

10   20   30   40   50   60 m

Jugendfarm Haidenwiese
Stuttgart

Index

1. Space in front of the gate; parking place for cars.
2. Narrow gate for people, wide one for vehicles.
2a. Garbage bin.
3. Parking for bicycles.
4. Wooden fence (because of the houses).
5. Manure dump.
6. Shed for lawn mower.
7. Garage for pushcarts and wagons.
8. Stable for animals that must temporarily be isolated as well as garage for trucks and carriages.
9. Paved road.
10. Treed field, to be developed into playing field for toddlers and their mothers; separated from the farm by a fence.
11. Shelter.
12. Manège.
13. Cage for rabbits and other small animals.
14. Nature reserve.
15. Play area for small animals.
16. Firesite.
17. Meeting place for the children's parliament.
18. Village and village square.
19. Townhall.

20. Wooden village fence plus entrance gate.
21. Construction wood pile.
22. Root cellar.
23. Porch in front of the house.
24. Communal space on the groundfloor of the house with two normal toilets, one large one for wheelchair patients and a kitchen.
25. Saddle and feed room.
26. Open stable.
27. Paddock.
28. Watering place.
29. Unpaved road (circuit for the carriages).
30. Slide, running from the upperstorey of the house.
31. Garden with vegetables, compost heap, and toolshed.
32. Riding area for the handicapped children; separated since the therapy requires a quiet environment.
33. Old street car serving as birdhouse.
34. Chicken coop.
35. Sheep stable.
36. Feeding place for the sheep.
37. Brick kiln.
38. Run for the sheep.

The spring of 1973 saw the official opening of this playground with the horse stable and riding lessons for "able-bodied" as well as "handicapped" children.

From that moment on, the place grew by leaps and bounds to reach the level indicated in the diagram a little over a year later.

Work on the village started in 1973, but the huts the children had built had to be torn down later that year because the site turned into a swamp whenever the rains came. The children, furthermore, discovered that one can not very well build a house without planning; therefore, the second attempt was much more regular and systematic with specific lots allocated for building purposes and maximum sizes for the houses prescribed. Each house has an address, including street name and number.

It goes without saying that the need for building materials and tools is constant and insatiable, and although part of all this is donated, a good deal has to be bought. The consequence is that the children themselves must supply at least part of the tools they use; the other pieces of equipment can be borrowed from the playground, one day at a time.

The management is in the hands of the children themselves. A firesite is located on the top of a small knoll, surrounded by heavy logs that serve as seats during campfires. But, more importantly, the weekly meetings of the "council" take place here; this council consists of two boys or girls as mayor and a number of aldermen, elected for two-week terms.

It discusses all questions dealing with life on the playground, including cases of vandalism; decisions are taken by majority vote, information passed on and viewpoints exchanged. Adults take part only in the meetings if the subject-matter requires their presence. Experience has shown that this Council possesses a great deal of intelligence, sense of justice and decisiveness, even in, and maybe because of, the absence of adults, although in matters requiring technical expertise, the presence of a counsellor is often necessary.

An interesting discovery was that, contrary to expectations, attendance during the summer holidays, rather than doubling, reduced to almost half of that during the school year.

The Haldenwiese receives about two thirds of its budgetary needs from government sources, primarily the city of Stuttgart; the rest comes from membership fees and gifts.

A number, such as the Youth Farm in Möhringen, have developed special programs for the handicapped; multiple sclerosis patients for instance come and ride the ponies, which are extensively used to provide exercise and enjoyment to a variety of handicapped children.

The results of these programs have been extremely encouraging, with marked improvement in emotional stability, social behaviour, body control, levels of anxiety, will power, and, maybe most important of all, the "joie de vivre"; the feeling of actually leaving the confines of the wheelchair, of being able to enjoy nature, of doing things that other children also do.

The Netherlands

The Dutch children's farms, or ***Kinderboerderijen***, are considered to have two primary functions, an educational one and a socio-cultural one. The educational function originates primarily from the concern for lack of opportunity to come in touch with animals as a result of urban living. Since the study of, and dealing with, living organisms is of great value for the personal and social development of children, this aspect needs to be part of the overall educational package.

The kinderboerderij provides the opportunity, through direct contact with animals and the right to handle and observe them, to get an idea how living beings function. These farms can also make a contribution to the development of a positive attitude vis à vis animals, nature, and the environment in general.

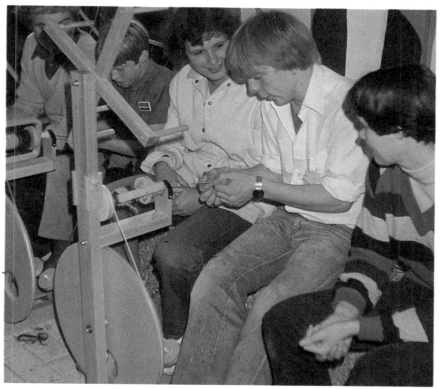

Speelboerderij Elsenhove – *Hans Schippers*

The socio-cultural function, based on the need for interpersonal contacts, is expressed through the fact that young and old meet; that the happenings of the farm provide plenty of material for discussion that helps combat the often increasingly superficial living environment, thus improving the environment in which the children grow up. The use of surplus space for creative activities, expositions by artists, or meetings of youth nature clubs, can be very positive, as can be the utilization of a kinderboerderij as consultation centre or animal-library, lending animals for educational purposes.

The cultural aspects can furthermore be strengthened through organizing other activities, such as musical performances on warmer evenings, spring-harvest and sheep shearing festivals, demonstrations of ancient handicraft, etc. The kinderboerderij can, during the holidays, become the centre for a whole series of nature directed activities.

It is important to realize that the farm must remain the centre, the focal point, and that the activities must never be to the detriment of the animals. The number and nature of the facilities that should be present at a kinderboerderij obviously vary with its purpose, local conditions, and available resources. The National Working Group on Kinderboerderijen of the Institute for Nature Protection Education has developed the following guidelines:

I.   **Basic facilities**:
- a stable with "farm character";
- paved square with cages for rabbits, chickens, etc.; seating for visitors;
- "meeting and cuddle meadow" that should also be accessible in bad weather;
- "rest meadow" with extra hiding space for the animals to escape too much feeding and too much attention;
- night shelter for chickens that are running around freely during the day time;
- provisions for pigeons in or outside the farm;
- dungheap.

II.   **Supplementary facilities**:
- "rabbit mountain" on or close by the square;
- duck pond with breeding area and feeding place;
- duck run on or close by the square;
- "colony cage" for raising chickens;
- small orchard with grass (as field for calves and sheep);
- garden for agricultural crops;
- field for wild flowers (for picking);
- vegetable garden close to the farm;
- breeding place (bushes) for songbirds;
- climbing opportunity for goats in the meadow.

III. **Facilities for a broader set up**:
- small playground for children;
- separate field for pony rides;
- tea house or similar establishment.

IV.   **Supplementary educational provisions**:
- spaces for classroom sessions;
- allotment gardens;

- garden for wild plants;
- bee hives;
- exposition space.

V.   **Other arrangements**:
- parking space;
- bicycle racks;
- superintendent's house.

Speelboerderij Elsenhove – *Hans Schippers*

One of the many children's farms is the ***Speelboerderij Elsenhove***, opened in 1976 and managed by the municipal government of Amstelveen. This is a real farm; the children are allowed, however, to help the farmer with his many chores. Adults too are welcome.

The farm is visited almost daily by classes of school children who come for practical classes in cheese and butter manufacturing, lessons on bees, nature and so on. The classes are conducted in the "Deel", the central space of the farm building which is used as a meeting place if no classes are being held. Special events include Easter egg hunts, sheep shearing and wool festivals, hayrides, cheese-making on Sundays, pony rides on Wednesday, Saturday and Sunday. The farm is closed Tuesdays, but open all other days from 14:00 – 17:00 h.

Other than the basic financial support from the municipality of Amstelveen, the work of the farm is supported by individuals and, from time to time, the business community; the revenue from these donations serves to finance special activities.

Sweden

One of the most comprehensive applications of the youth farm concept is the *Tolsered Junior Farm* developed in 1970 by the GAKO Recreation Community on a farm leased from the city of Gothenburg. The farm consists of a farmhouse, barn, storehouse, hen house and tool shed, and includes some 25 acres of fields and woodlands.

The uniqueness of this farm lies in the fact that, other than the usual participation in care of livestock and maintenance of the buildings, the visitors are also encouraged to help with the improvement of the farm and can share in the actural running of the operation. Thus, they obtain an insight into the real problems connected with the economics of managing a small farm. From this point of view too, the Tolsered Junior Farm differs from most others; it has maintained its farm character in all aspects. Another feature that deserves mentioning is the involvement of adults and old-age pensioners, together with children and youth clubs, in the overall project. This approach, and especially the involvement of the visitors in farm upkeep and improvement, has proven to be an excellent one. It has created a feeling of ownership, of belonging and of commitment that undoubtedly has contributed to the total absence of vandalism.

The program consists of the usual visits by individuals and groups, day camps during the summer months and educational tours from schools in fall and winter. Here too, a number of interesting features have been included. Family days, orienteering and special activities such as old fashioned Christmas celebrations, cooperative programs with museums and public demonstrations are organized on a regular basis. Very imaginative ones among these are the "Quiz Walks" which are some sort of walking bingo games in which also the partially blind can participate, since the figures on the cards are printed in braille. Other activities are also developed on the principle of integrating those who are handicapped into the overall schemes.

Since 1981, the operation of the farm has been taken over by the Recreational Services of the City of Gothenburg, in cooperation with the 4H clubs.

Environmental Education Programs

Environmental programs also range from those with a heavy educational emphasis, such as the Environmental Resource Centre in Edinburgh, Scotland, or those with agricultural-economic-overtones, such as the Seeds for Self-Sufficiency project between the Cub Scouts of the United Kingdom and the Scouts in Nepal, to those with an emphasis on community activities, such as the Washington Environmental Yard, in the United States of America. However, they all have an educational perspective in common, and all share a concern for the natural environment and the children's relationship with it.

Following the system established in previous chapters, the various projects will be discussed country by country, in alphabetical order. It must again be stressed that the examples are not meant to provide a comprehensive overview but rather a sample of some of the models developing in a cross section of countries. On that basis, we propose to deal with programs from Canada, India, Nepal, the Netherlands, Scotland, and the United States of America.

Canada

The program to be dealt with is called FOOD, *For Our Own Development,* and was developed in Bridgetown, Ontario. It addresses itself to grade six pupils of the Elementary schools and grew out of a Saturday morning market where young people sell products they have made, baked, grown, sewn or developed. It became evident over the years that there was a shortage of market gardeners; this became one of the reasons why the F.O.O.D. project was developed.

Its purpose is to encourage the children, hopefully with their parents, to establish and cultivate a garden, either for home consumption, to sell the produce or to show the crop at the local fair.

The schools participating in the project compete for the Green Thumb Award, presented to the school that has shown the greatest effort. The students receive instruction in how to grow vegetables, what the most common plant diseases are, what planting methods to use, how to use fertilizer and how to treat the various types of soil. The project started in 1974 and has since grown in participation and popularity.

India

The *Science Playground* in Ahmedabad demonstrates vividly that the development of play opportunities is in large part culturally determined and is strongly influenced by the socio-economic and demographic conditions of a given environment. India is a country with a really bewildering variety of socio-economic groups; its rural scene is vastly different from its urban environment. Within this heavily populated country the city of Ahmedabad is a heavily industrialized urban area dominated by textile or manufacturing plants. It is furthermore important to note that, in contrast to cities in the western world, Indian cities do not have organized playgrounds. Although some have informal play spaces, the recognition of playgrounds as an essential factor for the growth and development of children is only just beginning to develop and, therefore, the playground as a facility does not have a high priority in the educational system.

Science Playground – *Ling/UNICEF Photo*

One of the growing number of groups that have recognized this vital aspect in children's lives is the Vikram A Sarabhai Community Centre in Ahmedabad which, as one of its programs, has developed the Science Playground. The purpose of this facility is to initiate children to the world of science through a variety of outdoor activities.

The playground consists of a municipal playground, gardens, an exhibition hall, a library, a swimming pool, a science club, gymnasium, etc. and the equipment includes colour filters and mixers permitting mixing of primary colours, temperature blocks that can be used to give the children direct experience of the heat absorbing qualities of different colours and materials, a sound unit affording experimentation with sounds produced by pipes of different lengths, a machine area to familiarize the children with gears, pulleys and levers, and many more.

The basic objectives of the Science Playground are to motivate children to play, to provide opportunities for physical activity, as well as to experience simple scientific phenomena while at the same time serving as a model for the establishment of similar playgrounds in other areas.

Nepal

A project dealing with the same basic issues as those of the Canadian project is the one developed in Nepal called *Seeds for Self Sufficiency*. It is a "twinning project" between the Cub Scouts of the United Kingdom (8–12 years old) and the Scouts in Nepal, with the assistance of the Save the Children Fund. Nepal has a serious food shortage problem, in part because of its mountainous terrain, which is unsuitable for farming. As a consequence, plants must be grown on specially built terraces and special efforts made to cultivate as much of the available usable land as possible.

To stimulate the development of home gardens, the Cub Scouts of the United Kingdom help supply the seeds needed and each of the 24,000 Nepal Scouts plants his own garden. Some of the crop is eaten, but the rest is allowed to mature and grow seeds which are subsequently collected and stored.

At the same time, the Scouts tell the local people how to develop and care for a garden; they encourage them to start one with the seeds they have stored. The plan is that each of the 24,000 Scouts will in this way help one family per month to grow a garden. If this project is successful, 750,000 families will have been reached by the end of the first project cycle, which is 1982.

The Netherlands

The *School and Children's Gardens* in The Hague, instituted as early as 1919, are an important aspect of environmental education in the Netherlands.

Since that time, schools have developed their own school gardens to encourage children to take a special interest in nature because, even in The Hague many children are growing up in an environment consisting of houses, roads and factories, affording little or no contact with nature.

Dutch educational authorities put great stress on experiencing nature, and on developing good environmental behaviour because it is felt that "if the environment continues to be ignored, mankind may have no future."

The fundamental principles guiding the gardens are:

- Nature must not be shown to the students, they must discover it for themselves;
- First hand experience is more important than memorising facts and figures;
- Remembering an experience is more valuable than remembering what has been learned;
- Seeing interrelationships must replace repetition of facts.

Children's Gardens

There are two types of gardens: those the students work on during school hours, and those they go to after school. The latter are less structured and fall in the realm of leisure activities. Since 1971, nursery schools have been included in the school garden projects. They give very young students, from almost five years of age, the opportunity to sow seeds, care for plants and for small domestic animals, in special small plots.

In addition to the actual work on their plots, the children can attend demonstration lessons where they receive first-hand knowledge of the variety of plants and animals in their environment and are taught the interdependence of soil, atmosphere, plants (as producers), and man and animals (as consumers). These demonstrations also attempt to develop the children's ability to identify and understand a biological community and its relationship to its environment, the concept of the food chain, and the ecological balance.

Scotland

A very comprehensive program in the environmental category is that operated by the *Environmental Resource Centre* in Edinburgh, Scotland. The centre was founded in 1973, and its main purpose is to stimulate and support the development of practical environmental education in schools and communities. It attempts to achieve this objective by assisting schools, youth groups and community associations with the organization of environmental projects, by lending the required tools, by providing transportation, training and supervision, and by developing an information collecting and dissemination base.

The school-based projects the Centre becomes involved with include tree planting and related studies, the development of natural resource areas on school grounds, ponds, river and stream clean-ups, canal restoration schemes, air and water pollution surveys, nature trail layouts, coastal and sand dune conservation, wildlife protection, and many more. An example of a natural resource area within school grounds is that of the Riverside Primary School at Craigshill, where a large area at the school was planted with over 2,000 small trees and shrubs from a wide variety of native species, chosen to attract the maximum diversity of wildlife.

More recently, the Centre has supported and stimulated the formation of active project groups connected with youth schemes, adventure playgrounds, community associations and out of school clubs. In addition to these, activities for children with special needs have been developed.

All these projects, coordinated by local adults, consist of locally based environmental surveys and self-help improvement schemes, or are centred around visits to country parks and naturally wild areas of countryside. As part of these trips, the children are actively involved in projects such as tree planting, sand dune conservation and river clean-ups. Thus, these trips develop a sense of group identity and encourage them to be participants in the real world rather than be mere tourists and observers.

The Centre, which is an independent, non-profit agency, is for the major part funded by the Lothian Region's Community Education Service, with further assistance from the Carnegie United Kingdom Trust and the Queen's Silver Jubilee Trust.

The United States of America

One of the most imaginative projects in this category is undoubtedly that of the *Washington Environmental Yard*, Berkeley, California. It started in 1971 with an approximately one and a half acre asphalt schoolyard, flat, fenced in, and uninspiring.

Before and after at the Washington Environmental Yard – *Robin Moore*

   This piece of neighbourhood asphalt has been converted into a stimulating, responsive environment, intensively used by children, parents
and teachers on a joint school-community basis. The original asphalt yard
now contains three "sub-yards," an asphalt ball play area, a playground
with a large sand pit, modern swings, a variety of climbing frames and
cable drums, and a natural resource area with an informal garden, pools,
streams, beaches, paths, bridges, as well as some one-hundred and
thirty-five species of trees and plants, having attracted nearly forty species of birds. In addition, a small shelter and a well equipped potting shed
have been built.

   The construction job has mainly been carried out by students from
the University of California Colleges of Environmental Design and Conservation and Resource Studies, together with parents and children; the
material required came from a variety of public and private sources at the
local, state and federal level. Planning of the project was primarily done
by a leadership group, involving all segments of the community.

   The concepts upon which the project is based were developed following questionnaires, public meetings, observation and other communication techniques, indicating to the designers what children, teachers and
the community wanted. At later workshop meetings, these concepts
were thoroughly discussed with the potential users for further elabora-
tion, criticism and change.

   The initial phase, consisting of the removal of one third of the asphalt,
was initiated with a neighbourhood festival (yard fest) that has become an
annual event. The most difficult period came after this job had been
completed and decisions had to be made on what to do, where and why.
All this took time. However, throughout this period the area was used for
campouts, cook-outs and other events.

   As soon as trees and shrubs began to appear, a sense of community
developed – the yard became a rallying point for the entire community. It
has become the focal point for the organization of a large number of
activities: school classes spend entire days learning first-hand about

Washington Environmental Yard – *Robin Moore*

nature, celebrating birthday parties and taking part in summer recreation activities; during weekends the yard is used by local residents as a quiet place to read, sit in the sun, or play with their children.

But, in addition, there are days for construction, and building, because "flexibility" is one of the basic criteria of the yard. This and "open-mindedness", "access", "choice and diversity", guarantee a continuing sequence of growth and development of a process that has, in the ten years of its existence, become a model for innovative planning.

The project is managed by an incorporated volunteer group called "Friends of the Yard" and financed by the United States Department of Environmental Education, the California State Department of Education, and a special Environmental Education Fund of the California Licence Plate Fund.

Community building the Washington Environmental Yard – *Robin Moore*

45

The main reason for its success is undoubtedly the conscious application of the principle of involvement of the community at all levels and phases of the decision-making process. This has created a sense of community ownership, a feeling of belonging, and a level of interest and cooperation which otherwise would have been impossible to obtain.

The most recent development in the project is ***Project Plae***, Playing and Learning in Adaptable Environments, which is aimed at children with special needs for the purpose of demonstrating the impact of a diversified environment, such as the Environmental Yard, on the integration of these children into the community.

Project PLAE at the Washington Environmental Yard – *Robin Moore*

The method used is that of informal use of the Yard by these children together with the community. In addition, the project organizes special programs such as gardening, in which "handicapped" and "able-bodied" children work together, animal husbandry, providing opportunities to care for animals, and water play, consisting of supervised sessions with necessary wet suits and cushioning to enable children with contractions and able-bodied children to play together. There is, furthermore, adapted play equipment, a raised fire pit of wheelchair height for children's cookouts, a toy workshop and lending library.

We included the ***Children's Experimental Workshop*** in this chapter because of its emphasis on the natural environment as a major vehicle in motivating children with special needs in utilizing parks for the enrichment of their experiences.

During the six years of its operation, the program operated at Glen Echo Park, situated on the bluffs of the Potomac River, a few miles North West of Washington, D.C.

It used federal park resources to cultivate positive group interaction and to stimulate young people, "able-bodied" as well as "handicapped", to develop their own creativity while interpreting their environment. It consisted primarily of field trips, which provide the youngsters with first-hand experience of their natural environment aimed at expanding their attitudes and responses, exercising the imagination, freeing the emotions and developing the senses.

The objective of the project was to obtain diversity of expressions, understanding of the aesthetic and social contributions earlier cultures and ethnic groups have made, their different uses of nature, methods of

Project PLAE at the Washington Environmental Yard — *Robin Moore*

gathering and preparing raw materials and the processes they used to convert these into useful, decorative and ceremonial objects.

The expectation was that these approaches might lead to a broader based and more creative use of National Parks, especially by these children who had hitherto been unable to participate fully because of limited access as a result of social and physical barriers. Therefore, access in its broadest sense was the ultimate objective of the overall program and the method used that of arts workshops combined with field trips.

The material for the improvisational theatre, pottery, puppetry, music and speaking workshop was drawn directly from the story each park site, which the children visit, has to tell.

The workshops consisted of a maximum of 12 children at any given time; the group as a whole rotated between four workshop areas per day. Thus, a typical morning might include an hour of folk dancing and instrument making, followed by an hour and a half of batik. After lunch and a recreation break, the children might spend an hour acting out myths and folk tales, and an hour and a half making pottery.

To maintain a high adult-children ratio, at least one volunteer apprentice, and in many cases two or more volunteer assistants, worked with each child. The apprentices were chosen from college students and the assistants from the high schools in the area; they all followed a three day orientation program.

An important aspect of the work shop was its basic philosophy which stresses positive approaches to the arts, and the fact that the joy of creating is more significant than the result. Therefore, there were no formal evaluations, no winners and no losers; cooperation instead of competition.

In 1975, Glen Echo started full year programs, consisting of two 10-week sessions, meeting twice a week for three hours a day during the school hours. Although the Children's Experimental Workshop terminated its program in April 1978, we included it in this chapter because it provides an example of how the use of parks, be they national, provincial, or municipal, can be made more meaningful; how this use can be extended to children with physical, visual and learning disabilities as well as to those from a variety of ethnic backgrounds.

The Workshops have, furthermore, shown that with imaginative, creative effort and cooperation, parks can have a rich potential for learning as well as play.

Reference materials used in the preparation of this chapter include:

Kinderboerderijen, Landelijke Werkgroep Kinderboerderijen, Instituut voor Natuurbeschermingseducatie, Amsterdam, Netherlands, 1977.

Schippers, Hans. "Kinderboerderij, Doel of Middel", in *Mens en Natuur*, Amsterdam, Netherlands, De Volharding B.V., Vol. 32, No. 2, April, 1981.

Les enfants et la ville, Fondation roi Baudouin, Brussels, Belgium, 1980.

Brennende Probleme, Bund der Jugendfarmen und Aktivspielplätze E.V., Stuttgart, Federal Republic of Germany, 1977.

Die Jugendfarm Haldenwiese, Jungendfarmverein Möhringen-Vaikingen E.V., Federal Republic of Germany.

Knights, Kay. "City Farms" in *The Association of Agricultural Journal*, London, England, Autumn, 1977.

"Cardiff City Farm" in *City Farm News*, Inter-Action Trust, London, England, No. 7, 1980.

Tolsered – A Swedish Junior Farm, GAKO Recreation Committee, Gothenburg, Sweden, 1981.

"Learning to Care for the Environment" in *Ideas Forum Supplement No. 2*, Geneva, Switzerland, 1979.

Kothari, R. and L.S. Rao. *Science Playground*, Vikram A. Sarabhai Community Science Centre, Ahmedabad, India.

"Environmental Education and the Special Task of the Service for School and Children's Gardens in the Hague" in *Service for School and Children's Gardens*, the Hague, Netherlands.

Work in Progress – Annual Report 1979–80, the Environmental Resource Centre, Edinburgh, Scotland, 1980.

Harney, Andy. "Project WEY" in *Trends*, Washington, U.S.A., July, 1977.

Laurie, Ian. "What to do with an Old School Yard" in *Landscape Design*, London, England, February, 1979.

Moore, Robin. "Open Space Learning Play" in *New School of Education Journal*, Berkeley, U.S.A., Vol. II, No. 4/Vol. III, No. 1, 1973.

"A WEY to Design" in *Journal of Architectural Education*, Washington, U.S.A., Vol. XXXI, No. 4, 1978.

Moore Robin and Herbert Wong. "Washington Environment Yard" in Schoenfeld, Clay and Disinger (Eds.) *Environmental Education in Action – 1: Case Studies of Selected Public School and Public Action Programs*, ERIC/SMEAC, Columbus, U.S.A., 1977.

Ross, Wendy (Ed.). *Children's Experimental Workshop. Expanding the Park Experience to Children with Special Needs*, U.S. Government Printing Office, Washington, U.S.A., 1979.

Terry Orlick

Tom Zink

50

Games:
New Ways to Play Them

Games form a central element of people's lives. Their importance is felt throughout one's lifespan, irrespective of one's age and independent of one's socio-economic environment. Participating in games provides the individual with the opportunity to experiment, develop initiative, learn social skills, and perform at one's personal best. Games, for instance as part of festivals, are important instruments for a community to create a sense of neighbourhood, a feeling of belonging and an opportunity for contact between different age groups. And, at the societal level, games play an important role as carriers of cultural heritage, and as a means of maintaining an atmosphere of playfulness and creativity in a world threatened by suffocation in its quest for rationality and efficiency.

The "protestant work ethic," the "self made man" and an emphasis on the "bottom line" have made the Western World a highly competitive environment, where even games are apparently only attractive if a winner can be declared. The adage that "winning is not the most important thing, it is the only thing" has long lost its touch of the ridiculous, and become the trade mark of players of all ages and all socio-economic backgrounds. Even the simple game of Musical Chairs can no longer be played unless a winner is declared.

It was not always like that. For instance, Anatole France, in his book *Les dieux ont soif*, tells us about a party game called La chasse au coeur. Played by people of all ages in France, in the latter part of the eighteenth century, it closely resembled our Musical Chairs. In this game, the leader draws hearts on a number of objects in the room: one heart less than the number of players, who dance in a circle to the tune of a musical instrument.

As soon as the music stops, each player must run to a heart and put a hand on it. The one who is left out gives a forfeit to the leader in the form of a personal object, a ring, bracelet, scarf, or whatever. After that, the game starts again, with all players, and is repeated as often as time or inclination permits. When the game is over, those who have lost a turn redeem their forfeits by reciting a poem, telling a story, or performing an act to amuse the company.

The overly competitive nature and the segregationist and elitist tendencies of modern games have recently created, throughout Europe, North America and Japan, a number of reactions resulting in new approaches to games. The purpose of these new approaches, to which this chapter will be devoted, is to help bring back the notion that participation in games can, and should be, a joyous recreational experience in which neither age nor skill, but only the taking part is important.

The following programs came from Canada, England, the Federal Republic of Germany, Scotland, and the United States of America. They have many characteristics in common, for no other reason than that they found their origin in a similar concern. However, they show the influence of their respective social and cultural environments; therefore, the methods developed to achieve their common objectives are sufficiently different to make individual examination interesting.

Canada

In Canada, a program called *Cooperative Games* was developed in 1974. As the name indicates, these games emphasize cooperation and sharing, rather than strife and competition. They consist of traditional games whose structure has been changed, and of a number of new games, selected, developed or created for the opportunities they provide for fun and satisfaction. These cooperative games also provide the participants with the opportunity to know themselves better, to learn something about others, and about their relationship to the rest of the world.

Cooperative Games – *Terry Orlick*

Cooperative Games provide a play environment in which everybody wins and nobody loses, an environment in which people play "with" and not "against" each other, an environment from which the feeling of failing has been eliminated. The Cooperative Games are marketed by *Sports and Games Cooperatives,* an organization whose members have brought their message of cooperative play to home and school associations, church congregations, school teachers, recreation leaders, physical education students, and a wide range of other groups and individuals.

Some of the major attractions of these games are their adaptability and versatility. They require little or no equipment and are very inexpensive. They can also be used by a great variety of people and in many different places. Their flexibility permits rule changes whenever the situation makes this desirable. There are no specific requirements as to size of courts, the exact size and type of balls, bats, etc. The emphasis is on the concept, which is one of cooperation, sharing, working together; nothing else is important.

Musical Chairs is an example of a traditional game that has been changed into a cooperative one. Most of us will remember the traditional version. It consisted of a row of chairs around which the participants had to skip, walk, or run, while the music played. The key to the game was that there was one chair less than there were participants. As soon as the music stopped, everyone had to try to find a chair to sit on — one of the players was obviously eliminated. And so the game continued, the number of chairs being reduced after each round, thus producing, in the end, a winner.

In the cooperative version of this game the basic set-up remains the same. The music plays, the children skip around the chairs and, as soon as the music stops, they race for a chair. Again, after each round, a chair is taken away but — and this is the fundamental difference — no child is eliminated. Those who cannot find a chair to sit on, share one with somebody else. And so the game continues, producing in the end not one winner, but a whole bunch of happy, excited children, all trying to fit on the same chair. They are *all* winners.

An example of a newly invented obstacle game is Action. It looks in its set-up like a traditional relay race: two rows of children behind a starting line, facing a series of six different stations. The major difference from the traditional game is that each child, instead of trying to complete the course as quickly as possible, to assure a team victory, has to complete it in cooperation rather than in competition with the child in the other line.

The tasks the children have to perform at each one of the stations is based on this cooperation. For instance, at station one they must bounce a large ball back and forth four times, at station two they must jump rope together 10 times, at number three they do a front roll on a mat side by side, and so on until they have completed the entire course. The next ones in line need not wait till those in front of them have finished, but

Cooperative Musical Chairs – *Terry Orlick*

start as soon as these have reached station three. Thus a great deal of happy activity takes place, which is heightened when those who have reached the end of the course run back through the various stations to go to the end of their respective lines. Action, developed by the children themselves, can be changed, in a large number of ways, to suit the age and number of participants.

England

Inter-Action Trust, London, has developed the *Inter-Action Games Method*. It uses the overall operating principle of Inter-Action, which is to break down barriers of communication between traditionally segregated groups, such as teachers and pupils, actors and audience, amateurs and professionals, young and old, social workers and clients.

The basis of the program are communication games, consisting of a large number of old favourites which have become open ended and can therefore be adopted to whatever the individuals and groups decide to do. The old favourites selected, are games well known in most western cultures but, because the traditional constraints of age, class, sex and ability have been removed, can now be played by all people, thus breaking down existing barriers. Communication games can be used for a variety of purposes, ranging from therapy to entertainment; the primary objective is to secure the active involvement of the participants.

The sessions, which are held in small groups, have produced a number of beneficial side effects. They stimulate community feelings,

Inter-Action Games Method – *Inter-Action Trust*

social responsibility, self-discipline, self reliance, and the breaking down of ethnic, clan and temperamental differences. Each session begins with the players accepting the contract to play. This in itself is an example of the communication value. This means that the players understand and articulate the individual's and the group's responsibilities. Some players may not know the meaning of the word contract, but through doing the activity, and accepting what it involves, the understanding of the concept grows.

The method developed by Inter-Action makes communication a meaningful experience, especially for those who have always been reluctant to express themselves, since it fosters socialization, creativity and articulation, while at the same time strengthening the element of fun. The atmosphere of fun and complete acceptance, which trained group leaders are able to develop, encourages the active involvement of those who take part.

Perhaps the best way to explain the method is by describing one of the 250 games that have been developed. Music *less* Chairs, like Canada's Cooperative Games, is based on the well known musical chairs game. To play, everyone sits on their chairs, which are placed in a circle. The players are given numbers: one, two or three. To begin, each number group is asked by the leader to change places with other numbers of that group in a particular way: for instance, "all number ones change places acting like elephants".

The next step is to have all groups change places at the same time, all interacting in the middle of the circle, each number group acting out something different. This can develop into a more exciting game by introducing what is called the "cat-bird" seat. This is a special seat — anyone who ends up on it becomes the "leader", who must designate the characters or things to be acted out by the others.

Thus, all children have a chance to accept and experience leadership. Sometimes a leader fails, but in the atmosphere of the game this is unimportant. The child is still part of the game and can try again later on, gaining confidence along the way.

The Federal Republic of Germany

The West German Sport Federation, through its program Trimm Aktion, initiated *Spielfeste* as the latest addition to its arsenal of motivational activities. The purpose of the Spielfeste is to provide the opportunity to everybody, young and old, friends and strangers, families and individuals, to come together to participate in a large variety of games, with or without equipment, in which nobody loses but everybody wins.

The games can be held in a city park, a playing field, greenbelt, sportscentre or recreational facility. They have a carnival atmosphere with live music, refreshment stands, balloons, hats, colourful shirts and, most importantly, thousands of participants, demonstrating the popularity of the events. With their festive atmosphere, they fit well in the series of garden, forest and sports festivals for which Germany is famous.

Participating or spectating everybody enjoys themselves
Pädagogische Aktion   *Inter-Action Trust*

The Spielfeste are organized under the auspices of the Landes Sportbünde (Provincial Sport and Recreation organizations); other agencies involved in the organization are youth groups, churches, citizens' groups and others. The organizers ensure that all segments of the population are involved in the organization and staging of the event. The city cooperates by making the site available and by assisting with personnel, equipment, publicity and a host of other services. To provide extra publicity and attraction, the organizing committee secures the cooperation of a well known television or sports personality as Master of Ceremonies. The magnitude of the Spielfeste is shown by the up to one hundred activity leaders trained for each one. Spielfeste include a wide range of activities for all ages: games as diversified as balancing, bowling, three legged races, ping pong, bicycling, all kinds of ball games, obstacle races, hula hoop contests, mass-polonaises, rollerskating, human snakes, skate boarding and many more.

The nature of the games with their emphasis on participation, the carnival like atmosphere of the event, and the intergenerational approach to their organization, make these games ideal from a community integration and fitness promotional point of view. It is especially interesting that the organizers are able to obtain sponsorship from a wide variety of sources, not the least of which are the Landesbauspahrkassen (Provincial Savings Banks for housing construction).

Scotland

In Scotland, *Community Games* were initiated some 10 years ago by a group of people who were concerned that children no longer had enough opportunity to play and take part in sporting activities. Operating on the principle that all children, regardless of their ability, should be able to take part and to enjoy themselves, they used virtually all of the open spaces in their communities for a large variety of games. Often they had to be adapted to the space available. Although the Community Games are orientated predominantly toward sports, the emphasis is on the fun of participation rather than on serious competition and skill.

These initial games were so successful, that they rapidly spread across Scotland, an expansion undoubtedly fostered by their low cost, both in terms of leadership and equipment. They have now developed into a national movement in which some 500,000 children take part, sponsored by Cumbernauld and Kilsyth District and Strathclyde Regional Councils where the games originated.

The types and variety of games are only limited by the talents and interests of the volunteer leaders. They include, for instance, netball, field hockey, soccer, rounders, fencing, cricket and track and field. They are held primarily during the summer holidays in as many communities as possible. Over the few years of their existence they have obtained the active support of government, church leaders, parents, local businesses and social clubs.

Their success has made it necessary to hire paid staff, which introduced the delicate problem of how to maintain a balance between technically competent leadership and the so extremely important involvement of parents.The organization of leadership training courses for volunteers may provide the answer and serve, at the same time, to strengthen community involvement and leadership, which are seen as the basis for the success of Community Games.

One of the major advantages of Community Games is that they are held locally, often at the neighbourhood level, so that the participants do not have to travel to take part. However, games like these must be put in a realistic social perspective. They should not be seen as the panacea for all social problems. Undoubtedly they can enrich the life of the community, and they have proven to be a valuable instrument in overcoming the problems of identification, but they can never replace a well functioning, comprehensive recreational system, operating on a year-round basis or adequate provisions reducing social inequalities. Over the years, the Community Games have broadened their previously rather narrow sports orientation by including activities, such as painting and drama.

The United States of America

New Games originated in the late sixties and were the product of the pacifists and war resistors of the era. The intent of the first "happening" was to let people experience the source of war within themselves, by bringing them together on a large wrestling mat with the stipulation that anyone who was thrown over the edge of the mat would be eliminated. The game, accompanied by the music of a rock band, was intense and energetic, with a great deal of bodily contact but, much to the surprise of the players, it was also fun.

This was the beginning of New Games, which had their official inauguration in 1973 in a huge public event in which everyone was encouraged to take part, often creating and sharing their own games. The basic premise of New Games is that, by restructuring play, people can be given the opportunity to compete against themselves rather than against each other.

Everyone is encouraged to participate: there are no spectators, everyone is a player. Individuals, groups and families, all come together to take part in a stimulating and enjoyable recreational experience, in an atmosphere of cooperation, of sharing rather than hoarding. The guiding slogan, and the one everyone is expected to live up to, is "Play hard, play fair, nobody hurt".

The New Games, which in the late seventies were firmly established in the United States, with tournaments all over the country, need no special equipment, can be staged virtually everywhere, and have no or only minimal impact on the environment. The universality of the concept is demonstrated by the fact that it has obtained great popularity in many countries, for example in Sweden and Israel.

The attitude of playing together, which New Games hope to develop, is indeed central to the movement. The games are "new" in the way in which they are played — people compete because competition is fun and not because they want to win and the rules can be changed if they do not suit the occasion. Most importantly, in New Games "people are the most important part of the game".

The New Games movement in the United States is centred in the *New Games Foundation*, which serves as a focal point for the concept. It publishes material to communicate the concept because, without understanding its basic philosophy, one can miss the essential aspect of the movement, which is to have fun, to be really free, and able to express oneself.

The games carry exotic names, such as Tweezlie-Whop, Hunker Hawser, Lummi Stocks and Vampire. Because most of these games were created recently, names like these tend to be meaningless and not very descriptive of the games' content. A description of one of them may help illustrate the New Games concept. Out of some 175 examples, Lap Game may not be the most typical, but it does illustrate the potential of these games for mass participation.

Lap Game – *Tom Zink*

In Lap Game, all participants stand in a huge circle, shoulder to shoulder. Then all make a right turn and sit down on the lap of the person behind them. This can be done in two ways: the first is for one person to lay on his back with his knees bent — the next person sits down on the raised knees, forming a chair for the next person to sit on, and on and on until the whole circle is seated — the crucial moment comes when the person on his back is hoisted up onto the lap of the person behind him. The second way is for everyone to sit on their neighbour's lap at precisely the same moment.

The circle is more stable if people sit on each another's knees. Once everybody is seated, they may wave their arms or even try a caterpillar merry-go-round. The world record was achieved on November 9, 1975, in Palos Verdes, California by 1468 students.

General Observations

All the games and festivals described originated from similar concerns: the rapidly reducing play opportunities of the children of the industrialized world; the emphasis on competition and winning, rather than on cooperation and sharing that have become the major aspects of western games; and the lack of creativity, imagination and freedom that characterizes them.

The importance of these new approaches lies in the fact that they counter this "winner takes all" syndrome; that they stress the elements that threaten to be lost, but also put their emphasis on the role of the community, the importance of volunteer leadership, and on intergenerational contacts.

Once again, it must be said that these attempts to drastically change the nature of the games people play, *had* to originate in the industrialized societies. It is from those that the play element is in danger of disappearing; these are the societies that have deviated from the "natural pattern". That we are dealing with a deviation becomes clear when we study games in, what we often pejoratively call "primitive cultures".

Terry Orlick

People as far apart as the Inuit (Eskimos) of Canada's Northland, the Aborigines of Australia, the Papuas of New Guinea, and the Chinese of the People's Republic of China, all have within their repertoires large numbers of games that are based on the very principles which the new movements from the western world attempt to re-introduce.

Reference materials used in the preparation of this chapter include:

France, Anatole. *Les dieux ont soif*, Paris: Bordas, 1968, p.43.

Orlick, Terry. *The Cooperative Sports and Games Book*, New York: Pantheon Books, 1978.

Olsen, Sally (Ed.). *The Cooperative Games Newsletter*, Ottawa, Canada, Vol. 1, 1979.

Caldwell, Winn. "Ed, who is our Friend, Plays Games with Us", Inter-Action Trust, London, England.

Spielfeste, Deutscher Sportbund, Frankfurt, Federal Republic of Germany, 1980.

Stone, Rod. *Community Games Progress Report*, Cumbernauld and Kilsyth District Council, Scotland, 1980.

Fluegelman, Andrew (Ed.). *The New Games Book*, Garden City, U.S.A. Doubleday, 1976.

Terry Orlick

Robi Volta

Building Adventure into Play

Adventure is an essential part of growing up. By adding an element of adventure to their play, children learn to explore the unknown, to experiment with the unfamiliar, to test the level of their daring, and to recognize and evaluate danger. Adventure play, a natural part of living, teaches young children a good deal about themselves and the world they live in. Although it is still part of the urban world, it has become very unsafe, because of the rapidly increasing hazards; therefore, when we think of adventure play we generally think of it in connection with adventure playgrounds.

Although adventure and creative playgrounds are frequently used as synonymous concepts, they are fundamentally different in that adventure playgrounds consist of an environment primarily built and controlled by children, whereas the environment of creative playgrounds, with elaborate play structures and landscapes, is traditionally developed, designed and built by adults.

Adventure playgrounds operate on the basic concepts of responsibility and freedom; responsibility towards oneself and one's playmate – towards the natural environment and towards animals; freedom to create one's own environment; freedom to build, to run and jump, to make a fire or play with water, to garden or care for an animal, to laugh and talk, or to sit still and contemplate.

The equipment is very simple. It consists of used materials that the children, using their imagination and ingenuity, can recycle: scraps of wood, boards, sheets of plastic or cardboard, nails, hammers, saws and pliers, plenty of sand, and a continuous supply of water will do. There should be a hut, an empty railroad car, or any other type of shelter, to be used as office and for rainy days. There should also be trees to climb, a garden to grow things in, and a few live animals to care for.

But above all, there should be a playleader, who is really the soul of the playground; the determining factor in its success. The playleader knows the children, their strengths and weaknesses, encourages them

Building with adult-sized tools teaches new skills.

and guides them. He or she knows when to interfere and how to withdraw, and creates within the children a sense of ownership, of belonging, of community and, at the same time, of acceptance of an unwritten code of social behaviour.

The overall management and administration, including the responsibility for fundraising, the supply of material and public relations must be invested into a local Management Committee.

Because the focus of Adventure Playgrounds is the child and its need to experience, to venture, to create and to overcome challenges, their physical setting varies greatly. They can be found amongst the rubbish of bomb torn London or in Toronto's downtown harbour front. It is important, however, that they be fenced off to prevent vandalism or appease disturbed onlookers, but especially to help create the awareness and sense of community which are so essential for their success.

The atmosphere of an Adventure Playground is perhaps best captured in the following description of the one in Freiburg, Switzerland.

"An empty place, a lonely tent, a few truckloads of wood in the middle, a heart beats . . . . The next morning: the place is crawling with children. There is no longer a pile of wood – the place is covered with cabins. What next? A day later: discovery that we, adults, are the only ones to wonder what to do now the cabins are ready and the wood gone.

For the children there is no problem, they change the cabins, paint them, live in them, their "structures" are in constant state of alteration.

A constant supply of scrap materials is an essential ingredient of an Adventure Playground – *Pro Juventute*

We bring a new load of wood, the place attracts more children. They are not discouraged if a cabin collapses; they start anew, ask the older ones to help them, enjoy even the smallest successes. It is as if a fever possesses the children in the morning until the moment the tools are distributed; after that it is the enjoyment of always making something new. A small community develops. Stores and kiosks are opened. At night, cakes are baked and sold; competition develops. There are cabin chiefs and conflict between groups; but also a good deal of solidarity, friendship and mutual assistance.

We, adults, play our role in the background. Everything happens at the initiative of the children, we do not give orders, we do not pull ropes. We help only when it is necessary, when the children ask us. We make sure that there is some sort of general order, that leaves every one free to do what he wants."

Since their inception in Denmark in 1943, Adventure Playgrounds have spread to other parts of the world, initially in Europe. For instance there are over 250 such playgrounds in England and Switzerland has many Robinson Anlagen. The past decade has seen their introduction in Japan and on the North American continent, where, at the present time, a growing number have appeared in Canada and the United States.

Varying circumstances and needs have caused the development of a number of different applications, all strongly influenced by the cultural environments in which they originated.

For instance, a growing number is aimed at meeting the special needs of the handicapped, either by making provisions to accommodate and integrate them or by developing adventure playgrounds for the exclusive use of handicapped children. Some have established close working relationships with the educational authorities, involving frequent visits by classes; a number have combined the principle with that of the Animal Farm, and a few have experimented with Mobile Adventure Playgrounds.

The following examples were included in an attempt to illustrate the various applications and to provide a more detailed picture of the respective operations.

They feature applications from Canada, Denmark, England, Israel, the Netherlands, Scotland, Sweden and the United States of America.

Canada

The *Harbourfront Adventure Playground* in Toronto, Canada, is one aspect of the innovative development of Toronto's waterfront. The playground was officially opened in the summer of 1976 and, over the first two years of its operation, accommodated a total of 10,000 children, ranging in age from 3 to 16 years. Its daily attendance averaged one hundred children, half of which were composed of school classes.

Harbourfront Adventure Playground

While the program's basic approaches are common to those of many Adventure Playgrounds, an important aspect of this particular project is its growing capacity to accommodate handicapped children, thus making it possible for them to work alongside the other participants. Significantly, the playground leadership managed to interest the Toronto Board of Education in its philosophy, with the result that in 1977 a very success-ful joint program was developed for special education classes of local elementary schools.

Cooperation between playground leadership and educational au-thorities might prove to be extremely meaningful, especially in those regions of the world where population numbers and limited physical resources make it impossible to provide school attendance on a full day basis. The resulting combination of formal and informal education may well provide the multifacetted educational experiences that are basic to the child's growth and development.

Another interesting aspect of this Canadian example is its com-munity program enabling numerous day camps and recreational groups, as well as groups of children with special needs, including the blind, physically disabled and emotionally disturbed to visit the playground. Social service agencies dealing with children with various learning dis-abilities particularly found that access to the playground was helpful to them. This program showed that Adventure Playgrounds, acting as an integral part of existing social and educational services, can be most beneficial.

And finally there are the Playleadership Training Program, aimed at strengthening the quality of leadership, and the Volunteer Program. An interesting feature of this last program is that, through Mimico Correc-tional Services, the Adventure Playground received inmates who chose to serve their time by doing community service work. They assisted playground staff in building and repairing structures and participated in activities on the site. Community College students can earn course cred-its through participation in a practicum program at the playground, and numerous others assist with its operation.

Contrary to the majority of Adventure Playgrounds in Canada which have had difficulties operating during the winter months, Harbourfront has succeeded to remain open all year. Winter activities include chopping wood, making fires, cooking, making sleds and hockey sticks, curling, building with snow, and inventing games on the ice.

Denmark

Denmark was the birth place of the Adventure Playground when the Danish architect, T.H. Sorenson created, in 1943, **Emdrup** in the outskirts of Copenhagen.The original playground has since passed through vari-ous stages. After having been a place where children built, tore down and built again, it ceased to be a place of adventure with a highly mobile population. Instead it became a miniature village featuring little houses, streets and carefully maintained flower beds, built and inhabited by a stable population of children. More recently, the first of the Adventure Playgrounds seems to have reached the end of its life-cycle. The neat

67

houses have fallen to ruin, and the flower-beds are no longer maintained; the site seems to have reverted to its original state.

If this seems, on the surface, a rather discouraging development, it should probably be seen as the consequence of one of the major features of the Adventure Playground, namely that it meets the needs of the children of a given era and a specific environment. It is a strength rather than a weakness that it changes as those two factors change, demonstrating a dynamism that is lacking in the static traditional playground.

The second example from Denmark we want to discuss deals with the **Building Site Playgrounds**, interesting variations on the traditional model.

They provide the children, who always seem to be fascinated by, and present at a construction site, with a place of their own, a place where they can build like the real workmen. The Building Site Playground, connected with the construction project, is obviously temporary in nature. The materials used are scraps; the mobile toilets, facilities and workmen's shed of the site heighten the sensation that the builders deal with the real thing. Learning how to do things does not seem to be a problem; most of the workers do not mind spending a few minutes of their lunch hour to help them along.

This type of educational playground has proven to be an extremely useful environment to develop in children a knowledge of the various building materials as well as practical skills in building with tools.

Adventure playgrounds in Denmark are often established in new urban areas, at some distance away from the core of larger cities. One of the consequences of this condition is that children living in these dormitory towns do not get a good understanding of the way urban families live, and the older ones frequently lack exposure to other recreation opportunities.

Therefore, as an extension of the traditional Adventure Playgrounds, the clubs connected with the Danish Playground Association have developed a number of **Do-It-Yourself Workshops** where young people can construct go-carts, canoes, dinghies, and so on.

Making these articles has created new interests and motivated the creation of new programs, thus enriching the recreation experiences of young people while at the same time breaking out of the relative isolation of the adventure playground and establishing linkages with the broader aspects of life.

England

One of the most original Adventure Playgrounds is the one that was developed in 1955 on the site of the bombed out school in Lollard Street, just across the river from the Houses of Parliament in London, England.

On opening day, at Easter of 1955, the ***Lollard Adventure Playground*** still looked like a bomb site, with old foundations outcropping through the dusty earth and a top dressing of rubbish.

In time, guided by an energetic and resourceful Management Committee, actively assisted by a number of interested agencies and individuals, and directed by a staff of imaginative and dedicated professionals and volunteers, the playground managed to overcome its initial difficulties and grew into an exciting community for children of all ages, up to 250 at any given time.

Adventure Playground-England – *Play Times*

The program consists of a number of year-round events, such as workshops, an Old Age pensioners' scheme, and a magazine. Furthermore there is camping, construction and gardening, interspersed with a variety of games in the summer, with painting, modelling, music and other indoor activities in the winter.

The second example from England is that of the ***Angell Town*** Adventure Playground in Brixton. Plans for this playground were started in July 1968 and, by April of the following year, the playground was opened on an area of 1½ acres.

This too is a playground combining a number of features: there is the usual area with ramshackle dens, towers, climbing nets, rope swings and catwalks, but there is also a small grassy playing field, a small farm corner with a number of animals, and a garden adjacent to the farm.

The playground is staffed by a full-time playleader and an assistant. Attendance is by young children and teenagers, black and white; a youth club is the main user of the hut that adorns the playground.

Unique features of the playground are the pre-school playgroup for the under fives, supervised by the mothers, who also do their own fundraising; a mothers' club, meeting regularly at the club, running a keep-fit class and helping greatly with fundraising efforts and the organization of activities for the children; and an Old Folks' Club which meets one afternoon a week for tea, a chat, or perhaps a game of cards or Bingo.

Some of the mothers have come along to help with the latter club. Hopefully this may lead to a program of community service in which the children also might help by assisting older citizens with shopping, laundry and housework in case of illness or bad weather.

Chelsea Handicapped Adventure Playground – *Handicapped Adventure Playground Association*

In February of 1970, the first ***Adventure Playground for Handicapped Children*** was opened in Chelsea, England, for the purpose of providing a specially designed and equipped playground for children with mental, physical and emotional disabilities.

The materials available are the same as those for other adventure playgrounds; the staff consists of two playleaders, assisted by voluntary help, domestic help and a secretary.

The big difference between this playground and a "normal" one is probably one of scale. The number of children is smaller; they are frequently quite timid, and need plenty of time to adjust to the new environment. Much of the equipment is simple in nature, although very flexible, like sand, running water and plenty of open and closed spaces where a child can feel secure, can build its confidence, and a sense of adventure.

It is interesting to note that the needs and benefits of the varying groups of handicapped children differ only slightly. One of the major problems is that of motivating the more severely physically handicapped to move around, independently of adults and to indicate their needs and preferences.

As we have seen from a number of other examples, many Adventure Playgrounds include in their target populations children with handicaps, which raises the question of segregation versus integration. The tendency undoubtedly is towards integration or mainstreaming of "handicapped" and "able-bodied" children and adults; organizations dealing with the handicapped by and large agree with that principle.

However, the *Handicapped Adventure Playground Association* of London, England, while agreeing with the desirability of integration,

Chelsea Handicapped Adventure Playground – *Camilla Jessel*

feels that it is rare to see severely handicapped children join in the activities of completely healthy children in a playground. Providing Adventure Playgrounds for handicapped children provides them with the opportunity to attempt and achieve all kinds of activities at their own speed, without the competition of more able children. If their disabilities are so severe that they can never hope to play in public playgrounds, they have in playgrounds like Chelsea the opportunity to experience, to discover, and explore in an environment that is compatible with their potential.

Israel

An interesting application of the adventure play concept can be found in Haifa, Israel, where the Israeli Society for Disabled Children's Playgrounds has created *Gan Hayeled*, a sheltered adventure playground for handicapped children. Constructed within the confines of Gan Ha'em Park on Mount Carmel, the 15,000 square metre playground consists of a club house for year round activities, a number of slides, a jumping tower, climbing apparatus, labyrinth, bridges, ladders, sand dunes, and an area for creative activities.

Gan Hayeled Playground – *Brenner*

The Netherlands

The *Bouwspeelplaats* on the Zegwaartseweg in the city of Zoetermeer represents an interesting comprehensive approach to the provision of play opportunities.

The name construction playground does not really explain the nature of the facility because the construction aspect, in the sense of the building of huts, is only part of the many opportunities the playground offers. Other than the building site, there is an adventure playground with climbing towers, tunnels, plenty of water, hills, bushes and grass; a play yard with sandbox, caravan, children's gardens and monkey bars; a "cuddlegarden" with small animals; an orchard and play cabins the children can rent; a theatre barn that doubles up as theatre, carpentry hall, and indoor play yard; a canteen with office, warehouse, kitchen,

Bouwspeelplaats – *C. Brakel*

Bouwspeelplaats – *Gemeente Zoetermeer.*

tuckshop and toilets, and a large equipment shed. The activities are enormously varied. The children can build, look after their garden, groom the animals, play house, read, play cops and robbers, billiards, checkers, ping pong, and a host of other games.

Every Wednesday afternoon, and during the holidays, the leaders organize (in consultation with the children) special creative activities, such as handicrafts, animal grooming, maintenance work, sport and games. Although the emphasis of the playground is on individual activities, the playground also features a theatre group *De Vrybuiters* and a newspaper group that publishes the *Rommelburgse Courant*.

The leadership consists of a manager, an assistant manager, three leaders, and from three to six assistant leaders. Their role is one of motivating, stimulating and assisting.

The playground is accessible to children from 6 to 12 years of age. Although there is no admission fee, the children who want to use the playground must become members, which means that they receive a "building permit" which, in turn, allows them to borrow equipment.

The playground has developed a very interesting accounting system for the many tools, sport and games equipment it possesses. A child wanting to borrow a hammer, for instance, goes to the toolshed, takes a hammer from the rack and hangs a building permit in its place. Should somebody need two pieces of equipment at the same time, permission from the supervisors is required. This honour system appears to work very well and provides the leadership with an immediate check on the tool situation. The same system applies for the keys of the cabins which are small huts located in the orchard, if one or more chldren want to reserve one of these.

The large theatre-cum-play barn is an excellent facility for rainy days and provides enough space for a large number of activities at the same time.

On school days, the playground is open from 15:30 till 17:30 h and on Saturdays from 9:00 till 20:00 h; it is closed on Sundays and Mondays. The opening hours during holidays are from 9:00 till 20:00 h.

An interesting feature of this playground is that it operates a service to agencies and individuals. This consists of lending play materials, decorations or tools, but also, and more importantly, volunteering children and leaders to work on floats for carnivals and other community events.

This playground is owned and operated by the municipality as part of the youth division of the Department of Wellbeing.

Scotland

The *Children's Scrap Centre* is a very imaginative approach developed by the Leith Adult Resource Centre and implemented by the Lothian Adventure Playground Association in Edinburgh. It collects all kinds of materials: wood, tires, drums, paper, metals, plastics, rope, concrete, cloth, as well as paint, clay, glue and brushes. All this is stored in a large warehouse; the idea is that members of the centre collect what they need for their projects, whenever they need it.

Membership consists of organizations and groups working with children, youth, handicapped, and people employed in educational and creative play situations. The attraction of this approach lies not only in the fact that it offers an easily accessible and varied source of supplies, but also that it provides a focal point for the exchange of ideas, skills and experiences.

The Centre organizes, from time to time, workshops on the use of scrap materials, printing, building of play equipment, pottery, and the making of props and costumes for drama projects.

Sweden

Flatas is an Adventure Playground as a component of a Play Park. A Play Park is a relatively recent phenomenon in the Scandinavian countries and consists of an area, close to a given housing development, providing opportunities to the youngsters of that development to play close to their home. Play Parks are sometimes located close to a school for the purpose of integrating the school and the community and to avoid duplication of facilities.

The central element of the play park concept is the community and its main purpose to strengthen the sense of belonging and to develop a true community feeling.

At the Play Park of Flatas, a residential area in Gothenburg's south west end, an adventure playground has been incorporated into the overall facility which features tennis courts, badminton courts, areas for ball games, traditional play equipment, sand lots, a grass lot for animals, play houses and a place for indoor activities.

The Play Park is centrally located, directly connected to the neighbourhood's school and its sports ground, and forms part of the housing area. Traffic segregation is consistently applied. The parking lots are outside the built-up area with connections to the access roads and local streets. Thus, the school, play park and shopping centre can be reached without the necessity of crossing roads.

The lay-out of the park enables activities for all ages to take place simultaneously while still maintaining a community character, for each section joins into another and each is developed for a particular type of activity. This type of development enables collective events to take place as well as individual activities. The construction of the park's tool shed is an example of one such scheme; another is the construction of a giant roof to provide shelter in case of inclement weather.

A large central fireplace, surrounded by boulders and low seats provides an opportunity to learn how to make a fire as well as setting the scene for weekly campfires for parents and children.

The United States of America

A rather unique example in the United States is the ***Huntington Beach Adventure Playground***, which is located in an abandoned, city-owned, sand and gravel quarry, occupying about two and one half acres.

The site features a standing pond, steep bluffs for climbing and sliding, heavy foliage and some trees. The quarry walls provide plenty of privacy for the children.

The leadership is provided by the city, supplemented by volunteers from local universities, high schools and, occasionally, parents.

Nearly all supplies are obtained through donations; there is no special budget for these items. Donations are secured through articles in local newspapers, face-to-face contact with construction supervisors and lumber wholesalers, and appeals to service organizations. The overall cost to the city is almost the same as that of traditional playgrounds, primarily due to savings in the purchase of equipment, the cost of design and construction, and the lack of maintenance at the site.

The activities consist of the construction of huts and play apparatus, overnight camp-outs, dirt and mud sliding on slopes, tree house construction, rope swings, wading, rafting, fishing, gardening, fire building, cooking, and low organization games.

Injury rates at the site are comparable or less than at most conventional recreational activities the city offers. A 1974 study showed that the number of major and intermediate injuries was the same as that at traditional playgrounds; however, there was a greater incidence of bumps and bruises.

General Observations

From the examples discussed, but more specifically from the countries of origin, it is clear that the emergence of Adventure Playgrounds is an indictment of twentieth century urban living. It is an imaginative attempt to restore and develop within children the capacity to use imagination and initiative, to learn cooperation and self-help, to strengthen responsibility and respect, and to re-establish contact with their natural environment – all indispensible ingredients of a harmonious growing-up process. Modern cities, with their ever increasing populations and subsequently decreasing availability of space, have virtually lost the possibility of developing these facilities and therefore, Adventure Playgrounds are typical phenomena of large urban centres.

The large variety in their application is a typical example of the differences in available resources and specific needs; the projects chosen for this chapter are meant to give an impression of this spread.

In time, Adventure Playgrounds will hopefully become more readily accepted by the population and the tendency to hide their site at all cost will diminish. Countries like Denmark and Sweden, where Adventure Playgrounds are part of the social service system and therefore often attached to schools or close to settlements, should serve as examples in this respect.

The experience with the original Emdrup playground in Denmark should alert leadership all over the world to the need for continuous adjustment of operating principles, materials, and emphasis. "Star Wars" and electronics may well drastically change the Adventure Playground of the future.

Reference materials used in the prepration of this chapter include:

Zimmerman-Elsner, Ruth. "Terrains d'aventures à Fribourg in *Pro Juventute News*, Pro Juventute, Zurich, Switzerland.

1979 Annual Report, Adventure Education Concept, Toronto, Canada, 1979.

Lambert, Jack and Jenny Pearson, *Adventure Playgrounds*, Harmondsworth, England: Penguin Books Ltd., 1974.

Lorentzen, Borge T. "Building Site Playgrounds" in Arvid Bengtsson, *Adventure Playgrounds*, London, England: Granada Publishing, 1972.

Sigsgaard, Jens. "The Playground in Modern Danish Housing", in *Danish Foreign Office Journal*, No. 54, 1965.

Sigumfeldt, Max (Ed.). *Adventure Playgrounds in Denmark*, Danish Playground Association, Copenhagen, Denmark, 1981.

McLenna, Francis. "Report from the Angell Town Adventure Playground" in Arvid Bengtsson, *Adventure Playgrounds*, London, England: Granada Publishing, 1972.

Adventure Playgrounds for Handicapped Children, Handicapped Adventure Playground Association, London, England, 1978.

Whitaker, Dorothy. "Adventure Playground for Handicapped Children" in Arvid Bengtsson *Adventure Playgrounds*, London, England: Granada Publishing, 1972.

Starting an Adventure Playground for Handicapped Children, Handicapped Adventure Playground Association, London, England, 1981.

Bengtsson, Arvid. *Adventure Playgrounds*, London, England: Granada Publishing, 1972.

Vance, Bill. *U.S. Adventure Playground Report*, American Adventure Playground Association, California, U.S.A., 1979.

Karen Oster

78

Play And The Family

Throughout the industrialized world, concern has been growing about the integrity of the family unit, its cohesiveness, its ability to adapt, possibly even its continued existence as one of the basic institutions of society.

Since the early days of the industrial revolution, the family, in the sense of persons united through a blood relationship, has had to compete with other social institutions for a priority position on people's value scale. After the disappearance of the extended family and its replacement by the nuclear version, we have seen the advent of the one-parent family, the childless family, the reconstituted family and, lately, the fusioned family.

To these must be added the increasing variety of forms of cohabitation, with or without children, but typified by their absence of formal, traditional sanctions. If one adds to this the growing popularity of families in which both parents work outside the house, their often extended commuting times and, concomitantly, the increasing amount of substitute care given children, it need not surprise us that authorities, social service agencies and countless individuals alike, are becoming increasingly concerned about the place of the child in modern society; especially if one considers the pressures on the family unit exerted by modern day economics and mass media together with the growing influence of the urban environment on both parents and children. Integration and cohesion within the family unit have become extremely difficult as a result of all these centrifugal forces.

A phenomenon, felt most poignantly since the Second World War, that will undoubtedly play a major role in the near future is the diminishing proportion of children in most countries of the industrialized world whereas, in the majority of third world countries, children form the largest population segment. Clearly this will have far reaching consequences for the demographic composition of large parts of the world in the years to come. It is also clear that this phenomenon will seriously challenge the social and cultural fabrics of most industrialized countries.

The process of integrating young people into the overall society will become increasingly complex and difficult. Many countries already show clear signs of the problems involved; problems which frequently seem to lack solutions. A growing number of countries have recently turned to the family as a mechanism for this integration. The family concept, in this context, stretches beyond its traditional interpretation to include all people forming a household. The projects that will be discussed in this chapter are all examples of attempts to strengthen the ties within the family unit. They are probably more applicable to the highly industrialized nations of the world than to those which are euphemistically called "developing", and more prevalent in urban than in rural environments. They came to us from Australia, the Federal Republic of Germany, New Zealand, Norway, the United States of America, Uruguay, Canada, and England and will be discussed in that order.

Australia

The *Time Out* program, developed by the YMCA of Darwin, addresses itself to children 10 to 17 years old who are considered to be in danger of developing undesirable behavioural patterns or who are economically or socially disadvantaged. Its objectives are to provide recreation programs that aid the development of social skills and the feeling of self-worth; to provide opportunities for decision-making and development of initiative; to mix with peers and adults in a variety of social and physical settings; to act as support for the family structure; and to provide opportunities for the parents to develop recreational interests.

The activities consist of camping, excursions, riding, canoe making, disco dancing, involvement in Youth Needs surveys and Youth forums, community service projects, and many more. They are executed by groups of 10 young people under the guidance of a Youth Worker, meeting during the week as well as on weekends, depending on the nature of the activity. Parent participation has been extremely difficult to secure, mainly because of the lack of motivation and capacity to become involved in activities outside the home.

The most active level of community involvement has been through the school around which a given project is centred. The program has succeeded in involving young people who did not, or only marginally, participate in the wide range of community recreation activities as well as those who have considerable difficulty communicating thereby illustrating the social and educational value of play and recreation.

The Federal Republic of Germany

The *Familien Spiel* or Family game is an example of a game that need not necessarily be played in a family setting, but that lends itself extremely well for that purpose. A great many activities are excellent family activities without having been specifically designed as such, indicating that family recreation can happen virtually everywhere and at anytime.

The Familien Spiel, from the city of Munich, is based on the principle of a treasure hunt, combined with a tour of the city. The result is an interesting and varied tour of Munich that inevitably serves the purpose of helping children to know their city better. The game can be played by children and youth, up to the age of 15. They can play by themselves, in groups or, preferably, with their family.

Each participant receives a map of the city on which a specific route has been outlined; one can start at any point along the route, but must complete the entire trip because, along the parcours, at each of 53 different spots, a short question related to that specific place must be answered with one word. For example, when reaching the city hall, the question is "how many years have passed since this city hall was built?

The answer to all questions form the basis of a crossword puzzle which, if all questions have been answered and entered properly, produces a sentence. The children must furthermore write a short essay about an interesting or funny experience they had during the tour. All correct answers are eligible to win one of the many available prizes, and the best essays are published in a small booklet.

New Zealand

The *Get a Family Feeling* project is not a recreation program in the traditional sense, but a motivational one which merits discussion primarily for its potential application elsewhere. It started with the New Zealand Council for Recreation and Sport, an Advisory Board to the Minister of Recreation and Sport, appointing in 1976 a Family Recreation Sub Committee. This Sub Committee was born out of a concern for the decreasing contacts between people of different ages and, more specifically, the diminishing opportunities for intergenerational activity, and the increasing separation between the child's world and that of its parents, all consequences of the growing mobility and the greater individual independence that characterize modern society's lifestyles. Recognizing the important role recreation can play in bringing people of all ages closer together, and especially its potential of promoting family-centred activities, the Committee developed a Family Recreation Program that was launched in the latter part of 1970.

Its main purpose is to motivate local authorities, national organizations, clubs, as well as industry, to place a special emphasis on activities in which people of all ages can participate. Based on this principle, a large variety of projects have been developed, ranging from family recreation weeks, regular family nights in recreation centres, family picnics and barbeques, to family tree planting days, sports days, socials, and a host of indoor activities. The concept of a family is, for the purposes of this program, taken in its broadest sense including not only the traditional nuclear family, but also grandparents, aunts, uncles, friends and neighbours. Therefore, it addresses itself to all types of households, and all aspects of the community, and is intergenerational in the widest possible way.

Examples of the application of this motivational program are a Family Recreation week in Gore, a week of Family activity promoted by the municipal authorities of Christchurch, the designation of the Dunedin Festival as a Family Festival, and a regular Family Night in the recreation centre and pool promoted by the Kaweran Borough Council.

Family recreation activities are a priority in New Zealand –
Tom Zink   Padagogische Aktion

The Scout Association, Girl Guides, Boys Brigade, Girls Brigade, Red Cross Youth and St. John's Ambulance Cadets adopted the program as their major emphasis during the International Year of the Child; the National Mutual Life Association published a Family Recreation Calendar, as well as Family Fitness posters; a number of companies organized family picnics and barbeques; and some 70 Municipal Councils take part in a National Working Group on Family Recreation, which meets once a year to ensure that municipal policies are practicable and truly reflect local needs.

Norway

The *Pedagogical Play Centre* in Jondal aims at strengthening the home as the fundamental institution for the upbringing and care of children by providing the opportunity to families to play, read, do hand-icrafts, or any other meaningful activity together.

Each family chooses what it wants to do and how often it wants to do it. The prime objective of the project is to encourage families to do things together, to spend some time together. It is this last aspect that is considered the most important, because it is realized that parents often have so little of that commodity available for their children.

Although the Centre operates from a kindergarten, it is no kindergarten in the traditional sense. This format was chosen to make more efficient use of the kindergarten facilities and equipment during the time that it normally would be closed. The centre is therefore open in the afternoon.

Pedagogical Play Centre

Children up to 12 years of age are admitted, but only when they are accompanied by relatives. The adults are responsible for the children; they are the ones that must motivate and activate them since the centre offers no organized activities. The centre is also attended by mentally handicapped children with their parents, the ultimate objective being one of integration.

Activity hours are extremely flexible. Families come and go when they wish; grandparents and other relatives are welcome. As a result, the centre acts as a focal point for contacts between adults as well as between children. Fees are extremely low, especially if one considers that the centre also operates a free toy, games and book lending service. The bulk of the cost is borne by the Norwegian Government. The staff consists of a doctor, a social worker, a clergyman, a logopede, a psychologist, a toys and games leader, an education officer, and a teacher of special pedagogy. These people visit the centre on a rotating basis.

The project has been a great success, the number of participating families growing steadily. On the other hand, since the frequency of attendance was rather irregular, the size of the groups has been small.

In spite of special efforts, fathers have been reluctant participants. On the whole, as is the case with so many projects of this kind, this one too seems to be used primarily by those who would appear to need it least. Single-parent families, one-child families, or those with many problems at home, have unfortunately not availed themselves of the services offered.

The United States of America

The program we selected from the United States is *Let's-Play-to-Grow*, developed by the Joseph P. Kennedy Jr. Foundation through a joint project between the foundation and the administration on Developmental Disabilities of the United States Department of Health and Human Services. It is a program of play, sports and games for special persons and

Let's-Play-to-Grow — *Joseph P. Kennedy Jr. Foundation*

their families. It is unique in its emphasis on the involvement of parents, brothers and sisters, grandparents, surrogate parents, professionals, and volunteers in an ongoing program of play and skill instructions for developmentally disabled persons.

The implementation of the program has given rise to the formation of a rapidly growing number of Family Clubs which provide opportunities for family involvement and interaction including the handicapped family member. The clubs provide community support for handicapped children and their families as they arrange for parents to receive training in teaching and play skills and most importantly they open opportunities for handicapped children to learn and develop through play and recreation.

In order to stimulate participation by all family members in sports and games with handicapped children, a number of Guides have been developed covering a wide range of activities as well as additional resources.

The subject matter of these Guides are developed for the purpose of being applicable to special children of all ages. They can be used in all places under all sorts of circumstances, in schools, institutions, community centres, as well as the home, and can be an important vehicle to develop special children's ability to express themselves and enrich their realm of experiences.

Its purposes are:

● To enhance relationships among parents, siblings, and special family members, through shared activities.

● To stimulate the physical and social development, as well as the independent recreation skills of special persons.

● To improve parents' and siblings' perceptions of their special family member's worth and ability.

● To improve parents' confidence in their own ability to help their special family member grow through play.

● To improve the attitudes and skills of professionals and volunteers who work with special persons.

● To mobilize community resources to provide essential physical education and recreation services for special persons.

In recent years Family Clubs have been formed in Australia, Canada, Mexico, Puerto Rico and Venezuela.

Uruguay

The first project from Uruguay which we want to discuss is that developed by the Department of Camping Techniques of the YMCA in Montevideo. It deals with the *Family Camp for Pre-schoolers* which had as its initial purpose the strengthening of ties between pre-schoolers and their parents, and the improvement of the relationship between parents and kindergartens.

The experimentations started in 1968 with a camp in which 14 families participated. Between then and 1977, the program format and content underwent a series of significant changes. For instance, the original camps were very formal in their approach; they did not sufficiently recognize the parents' needs for rest, recreation and motivation, and the attempts to strengthen the relationships between the parents and the pre-schoolers threatened to exclude other brothers and sisters. Based on these experiences, later camps were based more on a recreational philosophy; attempts were made to avoid stereotyped activities; parents were encouraged to participate more actively in the program, and the tendency on the part of the professional staff to schedule separate activities was avoided as much as possible.

The fact that the councillor/teachers were provided with basic data on the family characteristics and on the role of each family member, helped greatly in strengthening the ties between the teachers and the families and in understanding the subsequent behaviour of the children in the classrooms.

These, and other experiments (some of which were exclusively for pre-schoolers without parents), resulted in the development of the principle that camping should become an integral part of the kindergarten curriculum, and that all family members should participate in this experience. It was found that this leads to a much greater interest on the part of the parents in the kindergarten program and an increased readiness to participate in its various activities. It was also found that the best time to hold such a camp would be at the beginning of the school year, although climactic conditions may make this impossible.

The format that emerged out of 10 years of experimentation is a camping situation in which separate programming and combined activities are blended. Parents are provided with ample opportunity for family recreational activities, but attention is also paid to programs of a more formal, more directed educational nature. The children pursue their activities under the guidance of the teachers, who become councillors and work in an informal way with the children, creating a friendly, warm and cooperative atmosphere. And, finally, a significant part of the camping experience is devoted to combined activities: parents playing with the children in a large variety of activities, ranging from treasure hunts, campfires, sports activities to story-telling and indoor games.

An interesting innovation on the camping theme are the *Camps with Grandparents*. The organizers felt that modern society, with its emphasis on the nuclear family, no longer allows close contact between children and the older generations. As a result, many of the opportunities to take advantage of the wisdom and experience of the elders is lost. Therefore, special weekend camps are organized to bring the children together with their grandparents. Apart from the prime objective of strengthening the relationships with the senior generation, these projects initiate in the child a sense of independence from the home environment.

Three programs, which may not quite fit the initial categorization of this chapter, but which do stress parent-child relationships, are the *Play and Learn* program started in 1975 in Toronto, Canada, the *Family Place* in British Columbia, Canada, started in 1979 and the *One o'clock clubs* initiated in 1964 in London, England. Because of their parent-child feature, we decided to include them at this point.

Canada

The *Play and Learn* Program operates on the principle that play can be an important medium to foster learning. Its second objective is to provide a model for integrating, in a pre-school setting, young handicapped and non-handicapped children who are, as much as possible, equally represented in groups of about 15, meeting two, three, or four half days per week.

Participation by the parents is an integral part of the overall program: they are directly involved, on a rotating basis, under the guidance of full-time teachers, trained in infant work and/or early childhood education, part-time therapeutic experts and a coordinator. They are also encouraged to attend evening meetings at which they can discuss issues of importance and relevance to them, and communicate with other parents as individuals and not exclusively as parents of a handicapped child.

Play and Learn – *Karen Oster.*

Most of the play materials used in the program consist of basic toys, such as rubber animals, blocks of various sizes, shapes and colours, dolls, water and sand. The children can use all of the available materials in an infinite variety of ways, guided by their imagination. Paint, paste and play dough provide further opportunities to develop their creativity.

The opportunity to participate in the program has been highly appreciated by the parents. It has fostered ongoing contact between them, has reduced apprehensions vis à vis handicapped children, and has greatly facilitated interaction between handicapped and non-handicapped persons. The project is funded, for most of its operating costs, by the Ontario Government and, to a minor extent, by participants' fees and by the Ontario Crippled Children's Centre.

Play and Learn – *Karen Oster.*

Family Place

The *Family Place* in Richmond, British Columbia is, in a number of aspects, comparable to the One o'clock clubs from London, England. It is a drop-in centre for parents and their pre-school children. While the children play with new toys, paint, dress-up or learn new songs, all under the supervision of a trained supervisor, the parents can relax, read a magazine or exchange views with others. The Family Place however is not a baby sitting service; the parents remain responsible and must remain on the premises. A number of Family Places have Family shops attached where good used articles can be purchased.

England

The *One o'clock clubs*, developed by the Parks Department of the Greater London Council, London, England, constitute a very imaginative and highly successful project. The Department had already developed a number of Play Parks for older children; however, during school hours these were virtually unused. In an attempt to extend the use of these parks and, at the same time, to provide smaller children with an opportunity to play away from overcrowded streets and heavily populated neighbourhoods, the idea was born to open the parks to children under five who could come to these with their mothers, fathers, or whomever takes care of them, to take part in a wide variety of play activities under the guidance of trained play leaders.

The clubs are open from 1:00 to 5:30 pm, every week day mostly on a year-round basis; the "caregivers" are free to play with their children, to sit and rest, or to talk with the others. But whatever they choose to do, they must remain in the area, for they bear the ultimate responsibility for the children. It must be clearly understood, therefore, that the one o'clock club is no babysitting service. As indicated, there is very little structure, no specific program, and no admission fee.

Each club is staffed by a senior play leader, an assistant and a trainee. The facilities of the clubs consist of an enclosure close to buildings where the children can play when it rains, and open play spaces with tables and seats where the "caregivers" can sit and relax. It is often part of the adventure playground of the Play Park, or a section of a community centre.

The clubs not only provide a healthy environment for the mothers to play with their children but, more importantly, they give the mothers a chance to discuss their day-to-day problems with the play leaders and thus enrich their understanding of their children, and their need to play. The absence of preplanned programs allows each club to determine its own direction; the activities, therefore, vary greatly, and range from fairly traditional games to caring for baby kittens, Christmas parties, demonstrations in road safety by policemen, and haircutting, as a special treat, from trained hairdressers.

Reference materials used in the preparation of this chapter include:

Harris, Adrian. *Time Out Program Report*, Darwin and district YMCA Youth Clubs, Darwin, Australia, 1979.

"Get a Family Feeling" – A Series of 5 Reports, Family Recreation Program, New Zealand Council for Recreation and Sport, Wellington, New Zealand, 1979.

Vagle, Mette. *Final Report on Pedagogical Play Centre in Jondal*, Ministry of Consumer Affairs and Government Administration, Jondal, Norway, 1980.

Let's-Play-to-Grow Kit, Joseph P. Kennedy, Jr. Foundation, Washington, D.C., U.S.A., 1977.

Zipitria, Gustavo. *Campamentos de Trabajo*, Associacion Cristiana de Jovenes, Montevideo, Uruguay, 1978.

Oster, Karen. *Play and Learn Report 1981*, Toronto, Canada, 1981.

Child helping to herd the sheep in Colombia

Play: A Social And Educational Medium

As the title of the book indicates playing, living and learning are closely related concepts. Every play project has an influence on the player's quality of living and educational processes; there would therefore seem little reason to single out a number of programs for their specific importance in these areas.

However, the uniqueness of the following projects is that they consciously use play as a tool to foster the social and educational development of children, and we therefore felt they warranted grouping into a special category. They deal with environmental awareness, special education or motivation to learn; some deal with community development, participation or counselling; others emphasize the importance of recreation for the total development of the child. It is interesting that many of the projects in this category originated in the developing countries, the "have not" countries from an economic and material point of view, countries where mere survival often is the highest priority of living.

This may be one of the reasons why play in those countries often has a utilitarian purpose; play and work are less clearly defined and more closely and intimately woven into the overall fabric of life, more directly related to the simple necessities of mere existence. Furthermore, the distinction between play, education and social development is often less sharp, more fluid.

The examples for this chapter come from Australia, Belgium, Colombia, Costa Rica, El Salvador, England, Hong Kong, India, Sweden and the United States of America.

Australia

Developed as an extension program by the YMCA of Darwin, the **Outreach** project is aimed at the aboriginal communities in Australia's

Northern Territory and meant to provide comprehensive recreation programs in this remote area. Its aims and objectives include not only the provision of enjoyable and meaningful recreational activities, but also the development of interest in the traditional aboriginal culture, an understanding and appreciation of aboriginal as well as european ways of life, training of aboriginal recreational officers, and an emphasis on the creation of community development oriented programs. The program is of interest because of its emphasis on local initiatives, participatory planning, genuine involvement of the aboriginal part of the population and regular, planned evaluation of the program's effectiveness.

The guiding principle followed by the Outreach officers in their contact with the communities is one of auto-direction and decision-making at the local level. They only become involved when asked to do so, and overall leadership is, as soon as possible, turned over to local management committees. Work in isolated communities, especially these where two or more fundamentally different cultures live together, is difficult and highly sensitive. One always runs the risk of being accused of destroying traditional cultural expressions and relationships, of imposing a particular value system on people who are relatively defenseless. To a degree, such an accusation may be justified, just as it is relative to the introduction of education or health programs. However, as long as those who advance these new programs and values are aware of the dangers and ensure that the new options are being presented as just that, and that the choice rests with the people concerned, the problems are considerably minimized. After all, culture is, in its basic form, "The way people feel, think and behave", which changes constantly, lest a culture become ossified and change into folklore. The important issue is to make sure that the people concerned determine the direction in which they want to go.

An approach as decentralized as that of this program obviously results in a wide variety of activities; ranging from hunting trips and arts and crafts, to basketball, soccer and softball. Financing programs like these is always a problem. Government, in this case the Northern Territories Department of Community Development, provides the core funding with the local structures raising the monies required for the various activities. This program, because of its method of operation and guiding principles, may provide a model for those who work in isolated, bi- or multi-cultural circumstances.

Belgium

Met Open Oog Op Weg, "Walking around with your eyes wide open", was a socio-educative campaign aimed at creating in young people a keen sense of their environment, enabling them to become better prepared for their future role in society. The campaign, developed by the Koning Boudewyn Stichting as a contribution to the International Year of the

Child, addressed itself to boys and girls between the ages of 10 and 17. The purpose was to encourage the children to observe their environment critically, to determine, as a group, how improvements could be made and to prepare an "observation file" that could lead to further concrete action.

One of the important aspects of the campaign, which was not a competition and therefore had no prizes, was that it provided young people with the opportunity to not only observe, describe and propose, but, above all, to put their recommendations into practice. It furthermore introduced the possibility of establishing meaningful contacts between the school and society at large. For instance, the subject of noise made it possible to study the hearing mechanism of people, the consequences of noise, as well as the discovery and recognition of sources of noise in the environment. Other projects dealt with the lack of play spaces, using the street as a play space, enlarging and using sidewalks, play in the natural environment, the creation of murals, organization of play opportunities and more.

Colombia

Ciadras de Recreacion "Recreation Areas", carried out in very poor villages or urban slum neighbourhoods, provides, once a fortnight, from May to December, recreation activities like handicrafts, dramatic arts, puppet and toymaking, folk dance, cultural films, group dynamics, field trips, sports and games. Its purpose is to make the respective communities aware of the resources they possess, to make the people of the communities conscious of the needs and interests of children and to develop community leadership.

The program is aimed at children of all ages, and special emphasis is placed on the involvement of parents and young adults. It was initiated by the Associacion de Guias Scouts de Colombia (Girl Guides Association) with assistance from the Colombian National Committee for the International Year of the Child and donations from a number of commercial firms.

Costa Rica

The*Children's Parks and Recreation Program*, initiated by the office of the President of the Republic is an excellent example of a cooperative effort between a senior level of government and that of the municipalities, while at the same time providing a strong incentive for community involvement and development. This latter aspect is possibly the most meaningful since it is based on a cooperative effort in which the municipal authorities, community organizations, together with parents and

Coronado Park – *Costa Rica*

their children work together with parents and their children work together on the construction, management and maintenance of play facilities.

The decentralized structure of the program enables the development of opportunities for play that are in tune with established needs and existing facilities. It consists of the construction of game and play equipment from discarded, recyclable materials and from prefabricated modules. The modules, which children can put together themselves, can easily be adapted to different situations and with slight reinforcements be made suitable for adults.

The program which was started in 1979 was extended in 1981, the International Year of Disabled Persons, to enable handicapped children to take part as well. This was initially achieved through the development of specially adapted modules to be used by children in special education centres. These adaptations consisted, in the main, of special access ramps and other protective devices. Since, the nature of the modules did not have to be changed, it made it relatively easy for handicapped children to play in the "regular" parks, as they had learned to feel comfortable with the modules.

The overall program has been extremely successful, 167 parks having been constructed within a period of two years.

One of the important benefits, other than that of providing much needed play spaces for children and adults, has been a feeling of ownership, of belonging and pride in the community, thus underlining their social and educational funders.

It is furthermore a testimony of the significance of active participation and stimulation on the part of a senior government in those programs that are of prime importance for the health and development of its citizens.

El Salvador

Concerned for the high percentage of children that fail to enroll in school, especially in rural areas, and the equally large number that drop out in the course of the school year, the Office of Basic Education of the Ministry of Education in El Salvador developed a series of **Recreation Workshops** for the purpose of motivating the children to come to school. The organizers attempt to involve parents in these workshops because one of the main reasons for the low enrollment figures is the lack of interest in and involvement with the school system on the part of parents. It was felt that significant improvement could be achieved if parents took a closer interest in the schools and if learning could be made more attractive to the children.

The method used is that of organized recreational activities, based on the workshop concept, and dealing with a large variety of subject areas. There are cultural workshops, dealing with story telling, poems and drama, educational workshops, teaching motor skills and expressive activities, physical workshops, with an emphasis on jumping, throwing, running and catching, but also workshops in mechanics, carpentry, tailoring and so on.

The leadership is provided by teaching supervisors, school teachers, community authorities, parents and workers.

England

Book Bonanza was organized by the British Section of the International Board on Books for Youth People, in the Pimlico school, London, to stimulate children to read by raising their curiosity and interest in books. For that purpose, 1000 children were brought together with 44 authors and illustrators, and 18 publishers. There was a publishers' exhibition, a bookshop, a bookswap, and demonstrations of painting and bookbinding in which the children were allowed to participate.

These latter activities especially were popular. The entire project was so successful, and the requests for repetition so numerous, that the IBBY, which is now represented in 40 countries, is seriously considering preparing an information package for application by schools, agencies and organizations around the world.

Hong Kong

The **Street Corner Children's Library**, aimed at publicizing the use of the library service to children and their parents, is operated by the Boys' and Girls' Clubs Association of Hong Kong in an attempt to counter the influence of the large amounts of detrimental literature available.

The immediate reason for the program was the fact that even children living a few blocks from their neighbourhood library seldom went there. In order to bring the library to the children, books were displayed at the entrance of residential blocks, consisting of multistorey apartment buildings.

Although the essence of the project is that it brought the library to the children and thus was not much more than a somewhat different application of the library concept, the environment in which the interaction is stimulated and the nature of the interaction itself, create an atmosphere justifying inclusion of the project in a book that stresses the play element in both living and learning.

The area used was about half the size of a basketball court; wooden boards provided seating capacity, and trestle tables the space to display books, pictorials and magazines. Advertisement and publicity were secured by means of leaflets sent to each household of the block, colouring and games competitions, posters and signposts. Volunteers were organized to help during the exhibition and Mutual Aid Committees provided extra chairs and tables.

The response was overwhelming: a total of 1,656 children, mostly between 6 and 14 years old, attended the afternoons and evenings of the four days. Some parents brought their children; all were surprised that the library had come to them. Later on, a reading corner was set up to provide a special space, since crowding became a problem.

Help Individuals Scheme – *Yang Memorial Social Service Centre*

The *Help Individuals Scheme*, sponsored by the Yang Memorial Social Service Centre, consists of a counselling service aimed at children who are not taking advantage of existing counselling services, either because they are unaware of their personal difficulties, or because they are not motivated to receive any kind of assistance.

To reach these children, a more flexible and dynamic model of service delivery, over and above the usual guidance and counselling services, was designed, aimed at developing their awareness of their problems and the confidence to tackle them.

The Help Individuals Scheme is made up of a group of devoted teachers. They are mature and have a genuine concern for young people. After some basic training in the psycho-social development of youth, the needs and problems of young people nowadays, as well as listening skills and fundamental counselling techniques, this group, with the assistance and support of the social workers, begins to make contacts with the neglected youth in the community. Contacts are made in a variety of ways, including home visits, outings, educational visits, leisure walks at the park, going to restaurants or the libraries, or any other place where the youngsters would feel secure or free to go to. Hence, a trusting relationship is established, aimed at giving the young people suitable guidance and care and helping them understand their own emotional or behavioural problems. In cases where the teachers encounter difficulties, or feel inadequate to deal with a problem, proper referrals to professional counselling service is made.

India

A movement that has steadily grown, attaining international status, is the *Balkan-ji-Bari*, which literally means "Children's Own Garden". Its motto is "Education and Entertainment" and its emblem is a rose. Balkan-ji-Bari brings children together in their leisure time for recreational activities, supplementing those in the home and at school. It provides them with a happy, joyous and cheerful environment, and enables them to live a full life and develop a harmonious personality.

Group activities are an important medium of the Balkan-ji-Bari organization; the children meet, if convenient, every day or, at least, once a week. The programs consist of exhibitions, film shows, dramatic performances, music festivals and sport meets. The youngsters go on outings and excursions, whereas the older ones go hiking and mountaineering. During their holidays they have the opportunity to spend some time at the seashore or in a mountain resort. The workers are almost all volunteers, who, periodically, take part in leadership training camps, conferences and seminars.

Balkan-ji-Bari also organizes Children's Libraries which, besides being book lending libraries, often organizes classes in drawing, paint-

Dada Shewak

ing, music, dance and handicrafts. All materials the children make or collect, as well as other materials of interest and educational value, are stored in Children's Own Museums.

The activities and programs organized by Balkan-ji-Bari are based on the belief that recreation is a medium of education in the broadest sense and that how a child occupies its leisure hours is an important determinant of the man or woman he or she is to become. Although the organization runs schools, these are not schools in the traditional sense, but rather places where the children select and practice activities of their own choice, suited to their aptitude. It is believed that in this atmosphere of freedom, culture and understanding, the children can indeed find their own self and grow to their full stature.

The creative nature of the Balkan-ji-Bari activities permits the children from slum areas of the cities, or the huts and shacks in the rural areas, to find outlets for self-expression. Apart from providing an impetus to their creative urge, it affords them an opportunity to mix, to know and understand one another better and thus to strengthen the feeling of unison and brotherhood.

Balkan-ji-Bari brings together children from all strata of society, irrespective of social status, caste, creed, religion or language. In a number of places it has developed Recreation Centres, Park Playgrounds, Hobby Clubs, Child Guidance Clinics and Parent-Teacher groups. It helps the homes for the deprived, unwanted, physically handicapped and mentally retarded children, distributes food, milk, clothes and toys to needy children, celebrates great days and festivals, publishes literature for children on child welfare, and raises funds for relief work whenever necessary.

Sweden

From Sweden comes the *Experience Workshop*, located in Sätra, a suburb north of Stockholm. Conceived by a small group of people in 1978, it was developed with financial assistance from the Swedish Public Inheritance Fund, the Swedish Council for Children's Play and the city of Stockholm.

The workshop, based on the principle that people of different ages, when provided with the opportunity to work together in joint activities, can establish meaningful relationships, is now housed in a number of maintenance caravans and a few wooden sheds. Most of the material used has been recycled and collected at a folk festival type market, with dancing, music and theatre performances as special attractions.

An example of the type of project the workshop undertakes is that of the construction of a water pump, built by school students during physics classes held at the shop. The pump is destined to go to Zimbabwe, thus providing the children with an opportunity to learn about physics,

Experience Workshop – *Jane Knight*   Experience Workshop – *Bengt Carling*

Experience Workshop – *Jane Knight*

Africa, cooperation, and sound and water energy. Other examples of items children build include a skate board ramp and a play house.

The workshop brings together children, students, unemployed youth, pensioners, parents and preschoolers; it involves youth centres, leisure centres, special welfare authorities, tenants' associations, the schools and the local police. The operations are directed by a joint committee, consisting of the various participant groups and the workshop staff. The program of the Experience Workshop includes excursions and summer camp.

The United States of America

The Central Pennsylvania Regional *Migrant Child Development Program* is a comprehensive program aimed at children of migrant workers for the purpose of closing the gap that separates their development from that of other American children. The reason for this gap (for the fact that, for instance, in educational matters, these children are various "levels" behind) is that they never stay in a given location long enough to take full advantage of the available opportunities.

The main purpose of the program is an educational one, "to ensure that all enrolled migrant students in central Pennsylvania are receiving educational programs and services necessary to develop self confidence, academic discipline and vocational competencies which can be used to seek, locate, secure and retain employment and to become responsible, productive and participating members of the community and society".

The means used to achieve this purpose, addressed to children from infancy through age 21, include family day care homes, group child and pre-school development centres, summer enrichment programs, remedial instruction, and after-school help. Beyond these career- and education-oriented programs, there are extensive social and supportive services in which parents are encouraged to participate in field trips, cultural meals, parent nights and others.

When one sees these children engaged in some of the many career-oriented skill training sessions, one realizes the close relationships that exist between playing and learning, both accumulating in life skill training. This interrelationship demonstrates itself still more vividly during the summer program that focuses, among other subject areas, on music, art and cultural enrichment.

The *Good Nutrition* program started at the Children's Hospital, Columbus, Ohio in March, 1975 for the purpose of teaching good nutrition to young children between three and twelve years. It involves members of the Dietary Department and of the Patient Activity Department working as a team. Each week one dietician has the responsibility of planning and supervising, with the assistance of the activity therapist, a lesson for the nutrition activity. All lessons deal with good nutrition in a play therapy setting; the number of children per lesson varies from five to fifteen.

In one activity, for example, foods were placed in a "mystery box" which was passed around so each child had the opportunity to feel the objects. After everyone had had a turn guessing what the various kinds of food in the box were, the children discussed the shape, texture and colours of the foods, which were then put in a large bowl and mixed with other ingredients. The finished product, a salad, was very popular and provided a social cooperative play session.

Another activity began with the dietician using plastic models of food for the purpose of discussing the four basic food groups. The children first classified the foods and then decided which foods would provide a balanced meal. Following this, they made collages depicting the different food groups. The children also made peanut butter, ice cream, milk shakes, cookies, bread, butter and roasted pumpkin seeds.

The response to this program has been enthusiastic and beneficial to all concerned: the dieticians acquired skills in working with children of different age groups; their increased understanding of children's capabilities at the various ages made them better prepared to develop diet instructions. The activity therapists learned a great deal about food composition and nutrition; most importantly, the children learned about food and good nutrition in an enjoyable environment, while at the same time enriching their experiences in the areas of fine and gross motor development, cognitive development, language and social skills, and sensory awareness.

General Observations

One of the most important conclusions to be drawn from the foregoing examples is that play can be used consciously to assist in the social and educational development of children; that play situations can be created for the specific purpose of developing those aspects. The emphasis may vary according to the prevailing cultural and socio-economic environments. Crowded conditions and economic hardship tend to stress the utilitarian function of play. Play under these conditions is frivolous unless there is a specific, almost productive purpose. On the other hand, the lines of demarcation are often less distinct in these circumstances; "play" and "work" do not operate in two clearly definable areas, but overlap, the one dissolving into the other. This in contrast to the industrialized society of which one of the major characteristics is its rigid structure, its attempt to separate the *Homo Ludens* from the *Homo Faber*, its tendency to categorize all facets of life. In such an environment, frequently reinforced by a dominating work and production orientation, games easily become synonymous with "a waste of time", something children like to engage in and adults only do when they have nothing "useful" to do; but with a guilty conscience.

Projects like the ones discussed help re-establish the unity that seems to have been lost and justify the hope that we may be approaching the condition in which man no longer consists of "physical man", "spiritual man" and "intellectual man" but has again become a whole and indivisible being.

Reference materials used in the preparation of this chapter include:

Outreach: A Recreation and Social Development Program in Aboriginal Community – Program Papers, Darwin and Districts YMCA Youth Clubs, Darwin, Australia, 1978.

Met Open Oog Op Weg, Koning Baudewijnstichting, Brussels, Belgium, 1979,

Proyecto Recreacion y Parques Infantiles, Casa Presidencial, Oficina de la Primera Dama, 1979.

"And the Children Wouldn't Go Home . . .", in *The Bookseller*, London, England, September, 1978.

Help Individual Scheme Report, Yang Social Service Centre, Kowloon, Hong Kong, 1979.

"Innovative Projects in Child Welfare and Development", paper presented by Hong Kong Council of Social Service, at International Council on Social Welfare Conference, Australia, 1979.

Weaver, Lynn and Diane Schlegel. "Planning a Nutrition Program for the Hospital Playroom", in *Journal of the Association for the Care of Children in Hospital*, Washington, D.C., U.S.A., Vol. 5, No. 1, 1976.

Uoreno, Rafael, Antonio. *Proyecto de Promocion y Recreacion Para Padris de Familia y nimos que no asisten a la Escuela o la abandonan prematuramente*, San Salvador, El Salvador, 1979.

"Experience Workshop" in *Swedish Play Council Annual Report 1978–79*, Stockholm, Sweden, 1979.

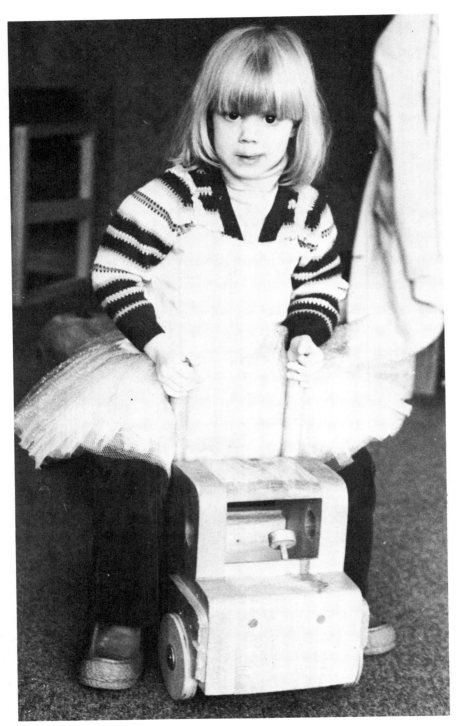

Toy Yard

Toy Libraries:
A Community Resource

I f one were to think of toy libraries as conventional book libraries dealing in toys rather than books, one would be in for a surprise.
Although both feature the name library and work with librarians, display shelves, membership cards, cataloguing systems, and in-and-out checking procedures, the parallel stops there. Instead of the sedate, almost academic environment of the book library, where even a simple sneeze often has the impact of an explosion, the toy library is characterized by an atmosphere of fun, gaiety, and uninhibited conversation. Toy libraries are a play environment where everybody gets in on the act.

Although the concept is not new (toy libraries have been in existence in California since 1935), its accelerated spread across most of Europe and North America is a rather recent phenomenon, starting in the late sixties and early seventies. Initially, toy libraries tended to cater exclusively to physically and mentally handicapped children and, frequently, mentally handicapped adults. For instance, the first toy library established in Sweden, in 1963, focussed on the special play needs of handicapped and mentally disturbed children, and the first one in the United States was founded by the National Institute on Mental Retardation.

In Canada too, the primary purpose of the first toy libraries was to help children and families with special needs. For example, the toy library opened in Hamilton, Ontario, in 1975, operated under the auspices of the Parents Council of the Cerebral Palsy Unit, and the one opened in Toronto, Ontario, in 1972, addressed itself primarily to the "disadvantaged" immigrant population. Thus, toy libraries originated in social service, attempting to equalize the play opportunities of children with special needs by providing access to toys; and providing assistance to parents, enabling them to respond more positively to their children's needs.

The toy libraries in Sweden have undoubtedly gone the furthest in developing these principles. The purposes of Sweden's over 60 toy libraries go far beyond the mere lending of toys. From the very beginning, the organizers have recognized the need to provide guidance to the parents of the handicapped and the mentally disturbed. This guidance helps them understand the special needs of their children and how to meet them. When necessary, it also helps them overcome any feelings of guilt or of having failed their children.

Besides counselling parents, the Swedish toy libraries, see their main functions as acting as an advisory bureau to parents; disseminating information to teachers, public health nurses and others; providing guidance to toy manufacturers; and, in cooperation with children's hospitals, researching the early detection of deficiencies or disabilities in children. Involvement with the children is, of course, considered of equal importance. Play is recognized for its value as a form of "work" in which the children can achieve a level of success as well as an important medium to train them to progress from one developmental stage to another.

The professional staffs reflect these functions. Where possible they consist of people with a strong orientation toward the development of children. Among these the therapist (*lekotekare*) is the central figure, testing the children, establishing whether they have the mental prerequisites for communication, and suggesting the toys that will be most appropriate for them.

Although many toy libraries in other parts of the world are still being established to meet the needs of children with special problems, growing numbers are now directing their services to all children, not just the handicapped, and parents who care to join. Consequently, in some cases, the operating principles, which previously had emphasized therapy, now emphasize sharing, participation and learning. A number of these libraries therefore employ "animateurs", specializing in motivation, who help the children discover new interests and develop hitherto unknown talents. Still others see toy libraries as a means of integrating the young pre-schooler into the (sometimes threatening) school environment, and of strengthening the ties between school and community.

All these developments underline the important roles toy libraries can play. They can be a major factor in the growing-up process of children, because they teach them to make intelligent choices as to which toys to borrow, to care for them, and to live up to their commitment to the library. They furthermore provide excellent opportunities to learn to play with others, especially for the only child. Just as a prospective book borrower has to look at a book before he decides to take it, so the child needs to have the opportunity to play with a toy before deciding to borrow it. Toy libraries therefore try to provide ample space where children can play with the toys and with each other. A growing number include books, games and songs in their lending items. This may help to establish the connection with book libraries and encourage the children to become, later on, users of those.

Toy libraries can also play a significant role in the integration of children into the family-unit through regular visits to the library together, and the opportunity of the mother, or father, to play with their children before taking a toy home. Toy libraries often serve as an informal gathering place for parents and other people who care to come and enjoy the children at play. In this way, they are an important element in the process of community integration and in the development of a sense of belonging to, and pride in, the neighbourhood one lives.

Many toy libraries include workshops where donated toys are cleaned and repaired, new toys designed and tested, and toy designers and the public have the opportunity to meet. Some maintain contact with their membership through regular newsletters, others use newspaper articles, local radio and television, and pamphlets to keep the general public informed. Various forms of membership and lending regulations have been developed. Some cover the children under the membership of their parents, others let the children join directly. Some levy fines for late returns, and others give a bonus for regularity. Toy libraries can be located in a public library, a community centre, a hospital, a day care centre, a nursery home, a play bus, or simply a private home.

Quite a few are operated by volunteers on a non-profit basis, although ready access to professional expertise is considered essential. Perhaps the most thorough approach to the preparation of staff is the Israeli one where "play officers", prior to operating a toy library, go through 80 hours of training. The financing of toy libraries varies greatly. Some exist entirely on membership fees, others receive support from service clubs, and again others are supported in whole or in part by a government agency. For instance, the Swedish toy libraries are supported as part of Sweden's national health program. Although a relatively recent arrival on the scene of play opportunities, toy libraries can be found on virtually every continent, from North and South America to Australia, and from Europe to most of Asia. The more detailed descriptions that follow are not meant to be exhaustive but merely to highlight some of the developments as they occurred in a number of countries. On that basis, short reports, appearing in alphabetical order, have been prepared from Canada, England, France, India, Israel, Mauritius, the Netherlands and Venezuela.

Canada

From the first one to be opened in Toronto in 1972, toy libraries spread rapidly across Canada, assisted in no small measure by the Canadian Association of Toy Libraries, founded in the fall of 1975.

The *Toy Yard* of Owen Sound, Ontario, operating since 1977, is situated in the children's department of the Owen Sound Public Library. It is a very comprehensive program, providing access to a wide variety of toys, a learning environment for both parents and children, a consumer's toy testing opportunity, a place for parents to meet other parents, programs for pre-schoolers, and a competent staff.

A play structure and display unit in one at the Toy Yard. – *William Waterton*

The toys are "housed" in two rather unique structures, with ample display space, which also give children an opportunity to explore, slide, climb and crawl. Most toys can be borrowed for four weeks, on the basis of one toy per child. The parents are held responsible for the condition of the toy, and a fine is levied in case of damage. The administration of the Toy Yard is divided into purchasing, cataloguing, cleaning, repairs, and promotion. Decisions on the purchasing of toys are made on the basis of answers to questionnaires that are distributed annually to all users. This survey gives parents a direct involvement with the Toy Yard.

An interesting addition to the services offered by this toy library is the Wishing Well Bed Box, provided by the Family Resource Centre of the Public Library. The idea behind these boxes is to provide play opportunities to children who are sick. The boxes are of brightly coloured plastic with a clamp-on lid that can be used as a lap tray. A typical Bed Box contains an idea booklet and most of the following materials: scissors, paper bags, note pad, colouring book, pencil crayons, glue stick, modelling clay, stencils, construction paper, collage materials, a deck of cards, hand puppets, a magnet, a magic slate, and library books. Anything the child makes may be kept; the left over materials must be returned to the library.

Another addition is a Pre-school Program for youngsters between the ages of three and six, meeting once a week for an hour of songs, crafts, stories and games.

An extension of this idea is the *Toy Lending Library* of Coquitlam, British Columbia. This unit is used by five elementary schools to reduce the risk of "first-day trauma" some children experience when they go to kindergarten for the first time. The parents in each school area are invited to take their pre-school children (ages between three and five) to the Toy Library at the school for an hour a week to meet other children and to play with carefully selected toys, which they may borrow to take home if they wish.

This toy lending program was started in 1975 to familiarize the youngsters with the school, but also to build school-community relations. It was also looked on as a method of improving the oral language development of the pre-schoolers through their association with other children, other parents, and members of the teaching staff. Another important advantage of this particular toy library is that a public health nurse generally attends the sessions. With this professional help, parents and teachers are sometimes able to detect problems in a child's mental, social, physical or emotional development.

The *Canadian Association of Toy Libraries,* organized in 1975, is a non-profit, voluntary organization. Assisted by an equally voluntary Advisory Council, it operates from a narrow, but growing, membership base. The Association plays three important roles, providing an information and resource service to its membership; acting as a consultant to toy manufacturers; and being a "watchdog" to ensure the protection of children from dangerous, unsafe toys.

The latter function is provided by a number of agencies, such as the Canadian Toy Testing Council, and the Product Safety Branch of the federal government's Department of Consumer and Corporate Affairs, together with the Hazardous Products/Toys/Regulations of the Hazardous Products Act.

England

From England we want to discuss two mobile toy libraries. The first one deals with the *Mobile Toy Library* in South Manchester. This started its operation in 1977 when an old double decker bus was purchased and converted.

It is a community education project, working with families and handicapped children. Other than a series of regular stops, the bus operates on a system which incorporates "request stops" in each evening run. Timings and routes are regularly evaluated and changes made whenever necessary. In an attempt to strengthen links with families which have difficulties taking advantage of the service, a pick-up service has been developed which brings those families to the bus.

The bus has a downstairs play area and toilet facilities; upstairs it has storage and display units, bench seats and coffee making equipment. The limited space on the bus makes a comprehensive display of the toys very difficult, therefore a rotating system has been developed. The crew consists of a driver/handyman, a nursery nurse and a part-time teacher, and, most importantly, the brothers and sisters of the handicapped youngsters.

A different application of the mobility concepts for Toy Libraries is the *North Hants Toy Library*, which uses a van to transport the toys to a number of locations, where the toys are unloaded, displayed in a church hall, school, or other such facility, and exchange takes place.

The *Toy Libraries Association* acts as the national headquarters of the over nine hundred autonomous toy libraries in England. Its functions include advice to groups wishing to set up a toy library. It maintains links at the national level with therapists, psychologists, teachers, toy manufacturers and other relevant groups and individuals. The Association publishes three times a year a journal, prepares and distributes booklets on establishing toy libraries and on children's development through play, and organizes conferences and special events.

France

Ludothèque 3CB – *Dominique Durand*

Under the auspices of the Carrefour Chrétien Culturel de Beau-grenelle, C3B for short, a toy library, *Ludothèque*, has been established for the inhabitants of the Front de Seine in Paris.

As was the case with most examples we discussed, this too has developed a characteristic of its own. Other than the toys a child can borrow, the Ludothèque encourages parents and children to participate in a social game which it makes available to them at virtually no cost.

The toys can be borrowed for a maximum of three weeks at a fee of between one and three francs, dependent on the nature of the toy; an annual membership fee of 50 francs is required.

Apart from the lending of toys, the Ludothèque offers, twice a week, an activity program to its members who are children from three to twelve years old. These periods have proven to be most excellent means of establishing contacts between children from widely varying cultural backgrounds. As a result of the overall objectives of C3B, which include offering a meeting place to people from different social environments, these twice-weekly programs have resulted in some of the most colourful and interesting intergenerational happenings one can imagine.

India

India, one of the most densely populated countries in the world, has a per capita income that is (in most cases) incapable of meeting basic human needs, and living conditions frequently unable to meet the most fundamental standards. In this situation Toy Libraries can play a very important role, allowing a great number of children the use of a large variety of toys and educational materials. It was on the basis of this consideration that the *Tricky Round Table* in Tiruchikapalli decided to organize a Toy Library in 1979.

Since this library was to be accessible to underprivileged children, it was located in an elementary school close to a slum area. The library, operated by a retired school teacher, assisted by teachers and students, was opened after school hours, on Sunday mornings, and during the holidays.

The unique feature of this library is that it is not a lending library, but the children come to play with the available toys. It's no wonder that the available space soon forced the organizers to limit admission. However, the success of this venture has caused other schools to organize similar units, and the municipality is planning to develop a recreational area.

Israel

The Israeli approach to staff development for toy libraries is probably one of the most formal ones. The *Toy Library Association* conducts 84 professional training courses, during which prospective "play officers" are exposed to problem-solving discussions, different games, parent meetings, matching games to the child's development, borrowing games, etc. Upon completion of these courses, the candidates become qualified to operate Toy Libraries.

The Association also assists with the organization of evening courses for parents, conducted by the play officers and spread over a two-month period. The purpose of these courses is to strengthen family interaction and to prepare the parents better for the crucial role of educators. Toy Libraries in Israel are mostly operated in schools and community centres, with the municipalities and School Boards concerned absorbing most of the costs.

Mauritius

The unique aspect of the *Toy Library Service* in Mauritius is that it lends educational toys and equipment to institutions, rather than to individuals. The idea behind this principle is that the toys, which are lent for a limited time, may be tried out and, if considered useful, copied. In this way, the service acts as "help to self-help".

The lending of toys is always combined with instruction, training, and follow-up. The service also supplies tools and know-how and assists teachers and parents in the production of their own toys and equipment

Experimenting with a new toy developed at the Embaba Centre, Cairo – *B. Gerin/UNICEF Photo*

from materials they have collected. It also plays the traditional role of lending toys to handicapped children. There too, however, the method of operating is rather unique. The service visits the families that want to borrow toys. Furthermore it provides, in collaboration with specialists, such as psychologists, physiotherapists, and specialists for the blind and the deaf, advice on how the family can stimulate the child.

These home visits follow a specific procedure, consisting of the initial contact through interviews and observation, the organization of activities in which both the child and its family participate, followed by training sessions with the parents, preparing them for their role in the process. These steps are followed by the actual lending of the toys and the setting up of a place in the home where the child and its parents can play. During this phase, the child is carefully observed for the purpose of, if required, the preparation of a remedial program.

Once this stage has been reached, special emphasis is placed on the socialization of the child by integrating it into the kindergartens, which organize "open houses" for this purpose. The last step in the procedure consists of the socialization of the parents, through meetings with other parents, teachers, etc.

The Netherlands

One hundred toy libraries, Speel-o-theken, are part of the *Stichting Speel-o-theek Nederland* which, since 1976 coordinates, advises, stimulates and supports speel-o-theken throughout the country.

Speel-o-theek — Mobile Toy Library – *Jane Knight*

One of these is the ***Speel-o-theek*** in the city of Leeuwarden in the northern part of the Netherlands. As with most other Dutch toy libraries, this one is not only involved in the lending of toys, but also provides information on toys and play, and is active in the discussions on play spaces for children and parents, inside as well as outside the home. Toys are loaned, for a minimal fee, to all those who are involved in the care of young children. The Speel-o-theek which has five distribution points is part of the Stichting Sociaal Kultureel Werk Leeuwarden and has no membership fees; toys can be borrowed at any of the distribution points, irrespective of the neighbourhood where one lives.

Each distribution point of the Speel-o-theek is operated by a neighbourhood group consisting of volunteers who meet at regular intervals to determine lending schedules, policies and so on. The overall direction is provided by a Board on which the neighbourhood groups are represented.

An interesting innovation are the Toychests stationed in various locations in the city. Toys from these chests however are not loaned to the general public but rather to the children belonging to the agencies where the chests are located.

Recently, the Speel-o-theek Leewarden acquired a Toy Bus, as a result of which four distribution points could be added to the existing ones.

A newspaper, the *"Speel-o-theek krant"* appears regularly to inform the population about the program items, how to make toys, and discusses various issues related to children and play.

It should furthermore be noted that the *Stichting Speel-o-theek Nederland* has structured a special task force to study ways and means of involving parents and children of different cultural backgrounds in the activities of the Speel-o-theeken. The result of this task force has been the publication of a booklet dealing with the major cultural differences, information strategies, past experiences and data on agencies dealing with people from other cultures. The need for a special approach had become evident because children from, for instance, Turkey and Morocco, must know and learn other things than Dutch children because their way of living is totally different.

Venezuela

The preceding examples show, in varying degrees, how the concept of Toy Libraries changes in accordance with the cultural and socio-economic conditions of the countries concerned. This conceptual adaptability is nowhere clearer demonstrated than in the following examples from Venezuela, a country that, in spite of the richness of its natural resources, struggles with problems of poverty and illiteracy.

One of Venezuela's ***Toy Library*** projects, implemented in a poor community in Ciudad, uses toys and the Toy Library philosophy to teach parents, and other adults within a household, the knowledge and skills needed to prepare their children for entry into the elementary school. It is not unlike the well known "head start" programs, operated in a large number of western countries for children who do not have access to regular pre-school sessions. The Venezuelan program is based on one developed by the Far West Laboratory for Educational Research and Development in California, in the United States. It is jointly financed by the Banco des Libro and the Corporacion Venesolana de Guayana.

The program centres around toys and games, lasts six months, and consists of weekly sessions to teach the adults how to use a given toy. After each session, the adults take the toy home; they and their children play with it for the rest of the week. They are expected to report on their experiences prior to receiving instructions in the use of another toy.

There are 16 toys in all and all are simple, wooden models, or sets of playing cards, each offering a variety of possible games. They are especially designed to teach mathematical concepts, and the recognition of colours, geometric shapes, common words and the letters of the alphabet.

The adults participating in the training sessions are primarily mothers, a few fathers, cousins, grandparents, and older sisters and brothers. The toys turn into a real centre of family activity, all members learning from each other, and, especially in cases where the parents are illiterate, they learn together with their children.

The success of the program outstripped the expectations by far. Not only were the children as well prepared for elementary school as those who attended pre-school classes, but the toys proved to be the means to involve entire families in creative, enjoyable activities. A similar use of the play concept for educational purposes was demonstrated when, in early 1977, the toys and games program was implemented in Caracas and operated from a small community library. Here too, the program was a big success to the extent that it has become a regular feature of the library.

General Observations

The examples dealt with in this chapter show that the Toy Library concept, over time, has developed in three directions:

- a number direct their toy lending and consulting services to handicapped children, and have a rather significant therapeutic content;

- others do not restrict their services to handicapped but provide toy lending to all interested children, and their families;

- others, again, have a broad community oriented program; involving toy lending, a play area, workshops, and informal gathering place.

115

In all these, however, we must remember that, important as toys are, they are only one element in the large and infinitely varied spectrum of tools, facilitating growth and development, to which the child must have access. As in the case of a balanced diet, a surplus of one ingredient can easily lead to partial malnutrition.

Furthermore, manufactured toys are but a supplement of the natural play material and should never replace the many opportunities nature provides. Prefabricated toys reinforce the consumer attitude and deprives the children of the opportunity to use their imagination and of the satisfaction of having made their own, crude as they may be.

The Swedish example shows that toys can be used as tools for a very special purpose. This applies to "normal" as well as "handicapped" children, as the example from British Columbia, Canada, indicates. These single purpose toys do not always have a long-term play value, and need to be replaced by others as soon as the objective of their use has been reached.

Toy Libraries play an important role in the education of parents. They have developed into a gathering place, in a way a community centre. They have strengthened family interaction; have been an important element in the development of leadership in the community; and have involved a large variety of people.

In spite of all these positive aspects, the Toy Libraries, like most voluntary agencies, do have to cope with a number of important problems, some of which are insufficient numbers of children, lack of professional support and guidance, lack of volunteer helpers and the means to develop their skills, poor facilities, difficulties in obtaining sufficient funding, and problems with toys.

Reference materials used in the preparation of this chapter include:

Lambie, Ruth. "How Sweden Trains Handicapped Children" in *Journal of Home Economics*, Washington, U.S.A., September, 1975.

Toy Libraries. How to Start a Toy Library in Your Community, The Canadian Association of Toy Libraries, Toronto, Canada, 1978.

Canada Works Project Report on Toy Yard, Owen Sound Public Library, Owen Sound, Canada, 1979.

Beckett, Barbara. "Is Heaven Like a Toy Library?" in *Canadian Living*, Weston, Canada, April, 1979.

Halton, Seth. "Coquitlam's Toy-Lending Libraries Help to Reduce First-Day Trauma" in *Education Today*, Victoria, Canada, Vol. VII, No. 4, 1981.

Biscoe, Lesley. "All Aboard!" in *ARK-Journal of The Toy Libraries Association*, Hertsfordshire, England, Spring 1980.

Palni, Tammy. "Israel's Toy Library – Boy Do I Envy Them" in *Canadian Association of Toy Libraries Newsletter*, Toronto, Canada, Vol. 11, No. 1, 1979.

"Round Table Toy Library in India" in *Ideas Forum*, Geneva, Switzerland, Issue 8, 1979.

Jaarverslag 1980, Speel-o-theek, Leeuwarden, Netherlands, 1980.

Speel-o-theken voor buitenlandse kinderen, Stichting Speel-o-theek Nederland, Amsterdam, Netherlands, 1980.

Meyer, Hanne. *Report on Joint Child Health and Education Projects*, Mauritius, 1977/78.

de Dearden, Carmen Diana. "A Library Toy Project in Venezuela" in *Wilson Library Bulletin*, New York, U.S.A., October, 1979.

Play Bus Rally – *National Playbus Association*

Mobile Play Opportunities

T he unique feature all mobile play opportunities have in common is their mobility. Their capability of being moved with relative ease, from one location to another, has added a new dimension to the provision of play opportunities. No longer are these dependent on whether or not the child can get there; no longer, therefore, are certain neighbourhoods, certain segments of the population deprived. The principle of mobility allows the "mountain to come to Mohammed", permitting the opportunities to be brought where they are most needed, thus making a significant contribution towards the ideal of equal opportunities for all.

Some use the concept to bring plays, pantomimes, films, workshops and other performances to a variety of public places. Others use the element of mobility as a unique opportunity to transport material to a wide range of potential play areas; others again, use a vehicle as a mobile workshop, containing all facilities needed to make it into a miniature community centre. Finally, mobile facilities are used as educational and resource centres.

All of these play opportunities found their origin in common concerns about increased traffic, sterile playgrounds, cramped living conditions, unimaginative play equipment, and growing passivity. All subscribe to the notion that play is essential for the development of the child and that therefore, the increasing shortage of play opportunities has become a serious pedagogical problem.

They are in essence motivational concepts approaching their target groups in an active and diversified way. They use old buses, delivery vans, fire trucks, trailers, refrigeration trucks, truck and trailer combinations and ordinary trucks; the programs consist of mobile playgrounds, toy libraries, arts and crafts, special projects and mobile shows. A number of mobile play programs have gone in a more specialized direction. For instance, in the U.S.A. Arts and Crafts vans, Puppet and Marionette vehicles, Sports mobiles, Zoo mobiles, Swim mobiles, Fashion mobiles and Teen Cantines were developed.

Other variations to the mobility theme are the Play Lorry, Radio Van, Mobile Printshop and Playcarts in England, whereas the Tea and Sugar train in Australia and the Swimming Pool Barge in Canada's Northland are imaginative examples of how to bring play opportunities to isolated communities spread over enormous geographic distances.

Playcarts – *Inter-Action Trust*

All of these programs represent very successful initiatives in creating flexible play situations. They are practical attempts to eliminate the lack of play opportunities and to foster the development of new, active and varied experiences in the day-to-day living environment of children and youth. However, when considering these positive aspects of mobile play opportunities, one must remember that they rarely can be considered long term solutions and in only incidental cases contribute to community development.

Mobile play opportunities ought to be seen primarily as motivators, as incentives to the community, as models indicating what can be done. The closer the ties with local groups and agencies, the better the chances that these will develop a feeling of "ownership" in relation to the mobile opportunity and the greater the likelihood that it becomes an integral part of the community fabric.

Mobile play programs consist of materials, vehicles and equipment; but that is only a minor part of the overall scheme. At the base of the project lie a series of educational concepts and objectives brought to life by the "animateurs", people who can put it all together, who can motivate children to participate in a large variety of play situations, who are able to transmit experiences through new approaches and material, and to bring fun and activity to places where the opportunities did not exist. After all, it is people who bring the mobile play opportunities to life.

The projects that will be discussed in this chapter come from the following countries: Australia, Belgium, Canada, Costa Rica, England, the Federal Republic of Germany, Ireland, Switzerland, and the United States of America.

Australia

Australia, characterized by enormous distances and low population densities, has specific problems in reaching its isolated settlements and providing these with the essential services.

The *Tea and Sugar Train* is a unique mixed goods train which travels weekly to the isolated communities in the northern part of the State of South Australia. The train contains a post office, a savings bank, water tanks (with supplies of city water), a retail store van and a butcher's van.

Once a month, members of the R.I.C.E. (Remote and Isolated Children's Exercise) travel on this train in a carriage known as the Community Service car. This is a fully self-contained carriage plus a second one divided into rooms where playgroups can conduct their activities. The purpose of these cars is to provide health, education, welfare and cultural services to the children and their parents in these remote areas.

The R.I.C.E. team consists of two teachers, a community health nurse, a toy librarian, and two part-time clerical assistants. Others who have joined the team include doctors, librarians (who read stories and perform puppet shows), personnel from Community Welfare, Family Planning, Mobile Museum Displays and Arts Council.

While the project, covering 250,000 square miles, is concerned with all children in the area, the emphasis is on those up to eight years old. The length of time spent at each settlement, construction camp, highway camp, or station, varies according to the population and the length of time required by the people to do their shopping. A typical range of activities includes medical advice, playgroup activities and a book exchange for adults and children. The project publishes three monthly magazines, namely *R.I.C.E. in Context*, *Tot's Turn*, aimed at parents of pre-schoolers and *Just for Kids*, for the five to eight year olds.

In order to meet the need for social contact with peer groups, weekend workshops are organized at stations along the track; parents and children from as far away as 200 miles get together for a weekend of drama, mime, music, campfire and crafts. Another innovation has been a 10-day holiday program for children living along the Transcontinental Railway Line.

The latest additions are the "Road-Rail" trips. These allow the visiting teams to spend longer in centres where more support and assistance is required, for instance, for the local playgroups. In these cases, the team travels by road and catches up with the train at a later time. Those trips may vary in duration from two to twelve days. Because of the enormous distances to be covered, a light aircraft is sometimes chartered to cover the far north east and north west of the state.

The overall program is supported by a variety of governmental agencies including the Commonwealth as well as the various departments of the state government, indicating the importance both levels of government attach to the program, which, by its comprehensive nature, touches on playing, living as well as learning, the three focal points of this book.

Belgium

Belgium is one of the most densely populated countries of the world. This condition obviously presents specific problems, one of which is a lack of play opportunities, especially in the highly populated urban centres.

Speelmanskarre – *Marc Huys*

The *Speelmanskarre*, operated by the Brugse Dienst Voor Speelprojekten, is an attempt to improve the play situations in the city of Bruges. It consists of a traditional caravan with a trailer, bringing a large variety of material, such as tires, crates, construction material, grease paint, makeup, costumes, and gas cookers, to playgrounds, city squares and streets, where the children, under the unobtrusive guidance of the four staff members, can freely play and experiment with all the "riches" the trailer contains. The caravan, which operates from April to September or October, visits the respective places from Wednesday to Saturday between 14:00 and 17:30 hrs.

Spelleketrek, operated in Brussels, is unique in the sense that it brings, apart from play opportunities, festivals, theatre, cinemas and workshops for "animateurs", thus combining in one overall project, three of the four models discussed in the introduction to this chapter.

Canada

Canada has many characteristics in common with Australia, especially those of distance and isolation of the remote areas. However, climate and topography dictate different solutions.

For instance, the absence of a railway network in Canada's Northland precludes the utilization of the train as a means of communication, and the scarcity of autoroutes makes the application of the play bus highly impractical. Therefore, imaginative planners went to the water and, with the financial assistance of the Canadian Federal Government and the government of the Northwest Territories, changed a large barge into a

"Corky" – Floating Swimming Pool

Floating Swimming Pool, complete with changing rooms, quarters for the instructional staff, purification system, etc. This barge was towed by tugboat along the MacKenzie River, visiting the small settlements along its banks, teaching swimming to children and adults.

The program not only provided an enjoyable experience to those who otherwise would have been deprived, but it also, in all probability, helped

reduce the rather high incidence of drownings among the native population. Unfortunately the river is, by the nature of its topography, unsuitable for aquatic activities. This, plus the short summer season, makes
swimming in the river virtually impossible. The success of the project is
demonstrated by the fact that a growing number of municipalities have
since built swimming pools, in spite of the harsh climactic conditions.
Thus, the barge achieved its main objective and could be retired.

The ***Touring Museum for Toddlers*** is another interesting attempt to
reach some of the most remote regions of the country. The uniqueness of
this project lies in the fact that it brings artifacts from the museum to the
children who are allowed to touch and feel them. This approach is a very
positive departure from the stereotyped museum with its image of
guards and chains, dominated by the "look, but don't touch" syndrome.
The project therefore, represents a new way of communicating nature
and science information to young children of pre-school age and is aimed
at stimulating among the youngsters an appreciation of the natural
environment.

The main problem was to design a program that suited the needs as
well as the capacity of young children between the ages of three and five
who are orientated to senses. They learn by seeing, touching, hearing,
smelling and tasting. It is through the exploration of these sensory
environments that young children learn about the world. This principle
became the basis for the development of the program which is presented
in a narrative way. The children are told a story, in which they are
encouraged to take part actively. They are encouraged to incorporate the
events they are seeing into their everyday lives. They are surrounded by
sound, pictures and objects they are allowed to touch.

The overall presentation, which lasts one hour and a half, is divided
into two parts. The first consists of a 30 to 45 minute play which uses
backdrops, costumes, puppets, film, slides and sound clips, all tied to a
narrative. Unlike a conventional play, the characters talk to the audience
and ask them to make suggestions on what should happen next. The
second part is a participatory exhibit, using artifacts, models, micro-
scopes and colouring sheets. In addition, bibliographies and suggested
activities are supplied to the adults, both parents and teachers.

The materials used for the presentations, consisting of electrical
equipment, a screen flat, a puppet flat and a display flat, are portable and
packed in the back of a van, which, in turn, is driven by the two project
leaders.

The project which, during its first season of operation in 1980 covered
some 20,000 km and visited 63 small rural communities, made 49 presentations, was attended by over 5,000 children and adults. It was funded by
federal and provincial government agencies, as well as the private sector.
The artifacts were borrowed from the collections of the National Museum
of Natural Sciences, which also provided administrative assistance.

Costa Rica

As with all projects discussed in this and other chapters, they reflect the socio-cultural environment where they originated. For instance, mobile possibilities developed in the highly industrialized part of the world stress the play element; those from countries where the distances are enormous tie them in with a more comprehensive social and/or community development package; and those which originate in countries with fundamental economic and educational problems, place the emphasis on these. They all have in common however, their quest for increasing the quality of the lives of those they aim to involve.

An example of a project with strong social and educational overtones are the *Mobile Units*, developed by the Patronato Nacional de la Infancia in Costa Rica. Its ultimate purpose is to fill the gap created by the lack of recreation centres for children and their families.

The program consists of mobile units, working in the outskirts of San Jose, with special emphasis on those sections which experience serious social problems, such as abandoned or maltreated children. The project leaders hope, through activities, to promote family unity and to achieve a better environment for the children to grow up in. The chief medium is play; games are used to prevent the children from getting bored and from losing interest; after the game is over, it is analyzed and discussed with them. Another aspect of the program is that of showing films to parents on the need of children to play.

One of the main objectives of the teams, which stay, on the average, one week in a given locality, is to involve agencies, groups and individual people of the community in their work. It is hoped that this type of program will prepare the children better for life, develop their initiative, encourage creativity and imagination, teach them to become part of their environment and to meet community leaders, visit other people involved in the program and thus, strengthen their sense of belonging.

England

The *Bristol Playbus* is a good example of a multi-purpose facility. This vehicle contains a toilet, cooking facilities, heating equipment, seats, running water, duplicating equipment, a public address system, sand pit, water tray and storage space.

The staff consists of two full-time people, who are both qualified drivers, a duty they share as well as the responsibility for the day-to-day project management and development. At the project office is a part-time administrative officer, and four part-time playgroup staff members, four arts and crafts instructors, as well as some 30-40 volunteers. The project is financed by grants and through a number of fundraising projects.

The children are organized in playgroups of not more than 16 chil-

Pre-school Playgroup on Play Bus – *National Playbus Association*

dren, taking part in a large variety of activities, such as puppet shows, screen printing, videos to develop drama activities, newspaper publishing and craft workshops. The bus offers a meeting place for mother and toddler groups and for language classes.

The following diagram gives an indication what can go into such a play bus.

This diagram was prepared by the *National Playbus Association*, an organization created for the purpose of assisting the more than hundred play buses in operation in England, Scotland and Ireland, and of providing valuable information to those who want to convert a bus into one.

The services include information on safety and reservation scheduling, training sessions at the annual conferences, discounts on gas and the lending of an "emergency" play bus in cases where the actual bus is grounded for mechanical reasons. These emergency buses (two in total) are also loaned to groups considering starting their own bus and needing a vehicle for a short period of time to promote the idea.

The Play bus concept has recently spread beyond the British Isles and Western Europe. For instance, the tiny sheikdom of Bahrain in the Persian Gulf has adopted it and, under the auspices of the National Playbus Association, a number of Bahrainian play bus staff has visited England to acquire first-hand knowledge of and experience with the operation of play buses.

An interesting variation on the mobile play theme is the *Islington Play Lorry*. This is a mobile adventure play structure built on the box of a

Cambridge Double-decker Play Bus – *National Playbus Association*

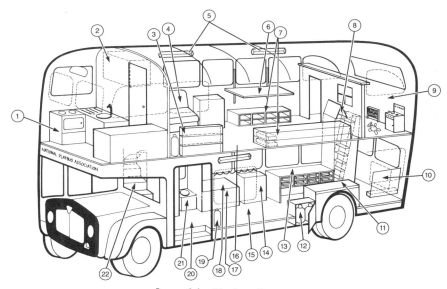

Legend for Playbus diagram

 1 Kitchen area
 2 Water Tank
 3 Book Corner
 4 Double Seat and Storage
 5 24V Strip Lighting (both decks)
 6 Adjustable Worktops
 7 Storage Units and Seating
 8 Fire Escape with Folding Hatch
 9 Dual purpose Wendy House and Puppet
    Theatre
10 Painting Easel
11 Sand Pit and Worktop Lid

12 Gas Bottle Storage
13 Work Surface and Storage
14 Catalytic Heater
15 Vinyl Floor
16 Carpet Floor
17 Puppet Window
18 Water Play Tray and Lid for Worktop
19 Fire Extinguisher
20 Power Operated Entrance
21 Toilet Compartment
22 Stairwell

three-ton truck, consisting of climbing frames, planks, flaps, nets, different levels, and a jumping platform.

The truck, with its staff of four full-time play workers, follows a regular schedule of after-school visits to neighbourhoods without playgrounds, where it is parked on any open space that is available. Other than offering the experience of an adventure playground, the project organizes craft sessions, outings and special programs. The crafts include leatherwork, tie dye, enameling, painting, batik and silkscreen. Special morning sessions are scheduled for the under five year olds; the staff also organizes play schemes during the summer holidays.

Interior of Play Bus
— *National Playbus Association*

Interior of Play Bus — *John Sani*

The truck cannot, and is not meant to, replace permanent facilities; its advantage lies in its mobility, in the fact that it does not have a fence around it and thus creates a real feeling of free for all. Another advantage is a motivational one; parents can watch their children, become involved and be encouraged to develop permanent play opportunities.

The project, which started its operation in 1976, was originally developed by the Islington Play Association, but has since become independent. It is financed by the central government through an annual grant received via the municipal council and is managed by a Steering Committee consisting of interested local people, such as play workers, a local social services representative, the project staff, and people from the areas visited by the truck. The Steering Committee meets every two weeks for the purpose of evaluating the project and, wherever possible, implementing improvements.

The *Kid's Radio Van* is a project developed by Inter-Action Trust, in London and consists of a mobile recording studio where children have the opportunity to make and broadcast their own programs. With the help from a team of experienced youth and Community Arts workers, the children, ranging in age from 6 to 17, devise, write, rehearse and record their own programs. The equipment of the van includes a silk screen workshop, which enables the children to print posters and advertise their programs. At the end of the day, friends, family and local residents can come and listen to the results on the radio.

The Radio Van spends up to three days on any one site; this period enables the children to become fully involved with the program, as well as with the Radio Van team. It also allows them to learn some of the techniques of researching, script writing and recording.

Kid's Radio Van — *Inter-Action Trust*

Through working on a "real game" project like this, the children also learn to articulate their thoughts, and to improve their socialization skills. It furthermore helps to de-mystify the media and to break down the feeling of alienation many have when faced with radio and other products of technology. Another important aspect of the project is that the children themselves decide on the topics. As they learn how to use the equipment, they determine their own texts and roles in making the programs.

When planning the development of a project of this nature, cooperation of a local radio station needs to be secured, funds for equipment obtained and, prospective playsites and Youth Clubs advised. Next, the schedule of visits must be developed and the staff that will work with the children selected and trained.

An interesting variation on the concept of mobile play opportunities are the *Playcarts*, also developed by Inter-Action. Rather than using mobility to bring a service to the users, as is the case with the other projects, the playcart itself is the medium, to be used by the children, worked on, altered, painted or whatever and, thanks to its mobility, able to be brought where it can perform its function best.

The basic ingredient is a renovated commercial garbage cart, which through imaginative use of colours, wood, cardboard, and other material, can be changed into a games cart, barbeque cart, jumble collecting cart, gardening cart and so on. As we said before, its mobility permits it to go where it is needed. All it needs is people to push it and the crowd will automatically follow.

Playcarts – *Alex Levac*

The operators range from pre-schoolers to 14 year old teenagers and the preferred activities are music, dance and the theatre. All material needed, such as arts and crafts tools, clothes for dress-ups, or food for a barbeque, go into the redecorated cart, and the project is ready to move. Steps in planning a project like this include:

- Contacting parents and tenants in the housing areas for the arrangement of dates, frequency of visits, help with refreshments, etc.;
- Working out names for the projects, methods of presenting the themes;
- Preparing the materials in easy-to-use kit form, ready to be put into the carts;
- Painting the carts and advertising banners;
- Devising appropriate projects for different age groups.

Experience with this project has shown that the secret for its success lies in its simplicity; the themes should not be elaborate, so that it is easy and attractive for the parents to continue their operation.

The Federal Republic of Germany

The West German applications of the Mobile Play Programs present themselves under a wide variety of names: the majority is called *Spielmobil*, but one also finds names like "Spielbus", "Bullerwagen", "Mobi", "Yuppi", "Rolli", "Mobile Spielkiste", and many more.

Jahrmarkt Spielbus – *Padagogische Aktion*

The first practical applications of the concept date from the early 70's, when in Berlin, Cologne and Munich, Spielmobile were developed. Since then, they have become permanent features in a growing number of cities with full-time staffs. The availability of qualified, motivated staff is crucial for an effective application of the concept. For instance, the Spielmobil in Munich, during the summer of 1979, did not reach its potential mainly because of staffing problems. Training sessions for staff are a prerequisite.

An interesting application of the Spielmobil concept is the *Jahrmarkt-Spielbus* (midway play bus) in Munich. It contains, apart from the customary equipment, five sections, namely: workshops, rental office, midway booths, tent and theatre. In the workshops children make the prizes for the midway and determine the content of the various booths. The prizes consist of medals, glasses, leather purses, bouncing balls, flowers, dolls, necklaces, masks, etc.

As soon as they are ready, the prizes are brought to the rental office. This is the place where the workers who made the prizes receive their wages (12 pfennig per hour), the booths are leased to the children, and the prizes distributed among the tenants. The midway booths, up to a total of 30, are constructed and operated by the children. A maximum time for rental of a booth (normally one hour) makes for regular changes. The activities offered in the booths include ring throwing, fishing, penny throwing and others.

Next, there is a large tent where the homemade prizes are exhibited and the visitors can buy soft drinks, popcorn, and other refreshments. An orchestra sometimes livens proceedings up in this tent. And, finally, there is the theatre, where a large variety of performances takes place. It is advisable to change these on a daily basis; for instance, the children can organize a fashion show, circus, dance exhibition, beauty contest, as well as normal plays.

In the meantime, and while all this is going on, or maybe at the conclusion of the midway, all the equipment of the play bus is used for a series of obstacle races, tug of war, treasure hunt, and other games. The "Jahrmarkt-Spielbus" normally remains five days in one location.

Spiel Aller Art Spielbus – *Padagogische Aktion*

Another interesting example is that of the *Spiel Aller Art Spielbus*, a play bus offering a variety of games in one location. The unique feature of this project is the "Play exchange" attached to the play bus where children can obtain information on old and new games, after which they can try them out. All these games are complemented by activities, such as the Theatre, Construction Playground and Workshops.

The following diagram gives an idea how the various games can be distributed over a given area.

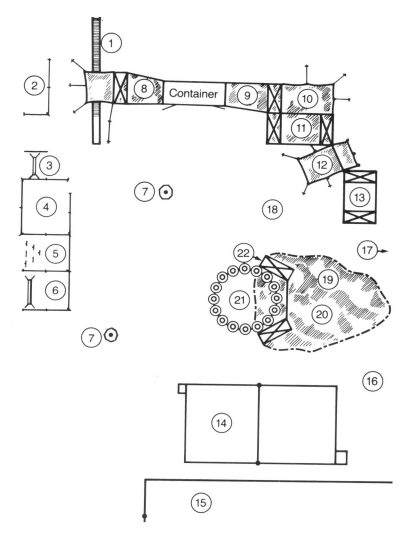

Legend:

1. roller coaster
2. construction playground with boards, cardboard, hammers, saws, nails, etc.
3-7. bowling, horseshoe pitching and others
8. equipment lending area such as balls, frisbees, stilts, etc.
9. space for the selection of activities; "Play exchange", parents corner
10. small games area, such as chess, checkers, dice throwing, etc.
11. theatre
12. workshop for repair and building of equipment, making of props, posters, etc.
13. climbing apparatus with ropes, tires, nets, etc.
14. playing field
15. running track
16. wading pool
17. playing field
18. table for painting
19. paddleball
20. life size dice game
21. arena, built with old tires or heavy rope; should be centrally located. Here games, wrestling matches and other spectator events take place.
22. administration

Experience with this type of play bus has shown that it is especially attractive for young children and recent immigrants; the games that are offered are not complicated and are internationally well known. The organizers also felt that the inventory of games must be kept highly flexible; the important aspect is that the available space is rationally divided. Colour in the overall set up is very important; the first impression the children get often determines their participation. Finally, long preparation time must be avoided; therefore, equipment must be kept simple so that the mobility of the entire operation remains assured.

Ireland

The *Dublin Children's Bus* is a double decker bus serving as a mobile facility. This represents a different application of the mobile play opportunity concept. Rather than serving as the container that brings the program to the places and children concerned, the Dublin Children's Bus itself constitutes the facility.

The original aim of the project was to provide pre-school education for children living in high density neighbourhoods with inadequate local resources. Based on this purpose, the staff, consisting of a Montessori directress, an assistant, and the driver, scheduled a series of 2½ hour sessions, one in the morning and one in the afternoon.

The program is meant for three and four year olds. Over time, it expanded to include parties and visits to the zoo, farms, the parks, and the ocean. Since it was felt that children and parents would benefit more if mothers and teachers would work together, the mothers were encouraged to organize community pre-school playgroups, and to follow pre-school playgroup evening courses. This idea was extremely successful. As a result the project philosophy has been changed rather significantly. Instead of offering a specific program, the bus has now become a resource centre, to be used by parents in their own neighbourhoods. The mothers now do all the work themselves, organize the participants, and buy the equipment and toys from funds they raise. Therefore, the Dublin Children's Bus Project, as it is operating now, evolved from a service directly to the children to a service to the parents, enabling them to enrich the opportunity for playing, living and learning of their children.

Switzerland

Although the idea for the Swiss *Spielbus*, operated under the auspices of the Pro Juventute organization, came from the West German Spielmobil, its philosophy and application have acquired a character of their own. Basic to the Swiss approach is the realization that it is not so much the play opportunity that has been lost, as the motivation and the

Spielbus – *Pro Juventute*   Spielbus – *Pro Juventute*

imagination to play. Therefore, the purpose of the Spielbus is to show those who live in a given neighbourhood, adults and children alike, how the available spaces, where people live, right next door to the house, can be used to reactivate spontaneity and imagination, not with expensive equipment, but with ideas and all kinds of material, often surplus, discarded items.

Therefore, the Spielbus is not a mobile playroom, but a van, transporting material, old tires, balls, paint, paper, etc. The people on the van are not babysitters but "animateurs"; their job is to stimulate creativity, to search for possibilities, not only within the children, but also within the parents. Their role is to reinforce and stimulate the process of discovery that must be carried, developed, and above all, understood by the people of the neighbourhood.

The intent is to bring the play atmosphere back to where the people live. The initiators realize that the child's freedom to play cannot be enhanced simply by calling for more playgrounds, or by providing more space, but rather by recognizing and rediscovering play next to the front door and around the corner, by helping the child regain its ancestral preserve around the house and in the neighbourhood. To achieve this, not only the children must be educated, but also the grown ups.

The Spielbus does not arrive in a given neighbourhood with a planned program, as is the case in a number of other examples, but with as large a variety of material as possible, ready to respond to the most diverse situations and demands.

The leaders have learned that children's play cannot be structured, that the visits of the bus are meaningless unless they serve to discover play spaces, and to experience the feeling of community. This can be brought about through the initiatives of children and their parents, and through showing that the quality of play cannot be measured in terms of square metres, but that it depends on the opportunity to experience creativity, on imaginative initiatives, and on an adult world that understands that who can play, learns to live.

Robinson Kinderzircus – *Pro Juventute*

A popular phenomenon, especially in the western European countries, are the children's circuses, the most sophisticated one probably being the ***Robinson Kinderzircus***, born out of one of the recreation centres in Zurich and now a separate department of its Friezeitanlagen (Recreation centers) This circus, which celebrated its twentieth anniversary in 1980, has, since the fall of 1979, secured its own permanent quarters, provided by the city of Zurich. It becomes mobile during its annual three week tour to a number of Swiss towns and cities.

Robinson Kinderzircus – *Pro Juventute*

The circus has its own director, who is assisted by a Parent Committee. This committee looks after all publicity, including contacts with the press, graphics, printing of programs, etc. Its members are also actively involved in management and organization of the project; many parents volunteer to set up the heavy equipment and to make the costumes.

The program of the Kinderzircus, in which some 40 to 50 children, between the ages of 5 and 16, participate, includes clowns, acrobats, animal trainers, magicians, trapeze artists and many more. Interestingly, the children show a strong allegiance to their circus; the average lifespan of the artists is four or five years.

The policy is to operate on a break even principle; however, rising costs and sometimes inclement weather makes this not always possible. The city of Zurich has, in these cases, absorbed the deficit.

The United States of America

The concept of mobile recreation programs was applied in Nassau County, in the state of New York as early as 1968. Initially, the programs were directed at children and limited to the summer months. However, in time and with an increase in the number of cities applying the concept, its scope broadened so that at the present time the mobile play opportunities are directed at all age groups and frequently on a year-round basis.

Community involvement in planning, design and evaluation of the projects is central to its success. Unless cooperation and commitment from those who live in the areas visited can be obtained, the mobile play concept remains alien and superimposed, and its benefits will not go beyond those of any other "consumption" item. Therefore, organizers must develop a system of close liaison with the population concerned and with the recreation and social service agencies of the neighbourhood. Participation by all of these must include involvement in arranging crowd control, cooperation with the police, advertising, as well as procurement of special equipment, such as toilets for the participants, emergency telephone and so on.

Skate Mobile – *Fran Wallach*

The Nassau county mobile units include a *Skate mobile*, including a commercial sweeper (to clean the area) and spotlights for evening programs; a *Fashion mobile*, offering sewing, hairstyling, make-up and instructions on good grooming and fashion; a *Mini mobile*, offering story books, paper backs, and large print books for the visually impaired; a

Teen canteen with live bands playing from a stage at the rear of the unit, and soft drinks dispensed from the serving area at the front; a *Show wagon* for the performing arts; a *Craft mobile*, complete with potter's wheels and electric kilns; a *Sports mobile* for physical fitness and sports activities, and a *Puppet theatre*, offering puppet shows.

The mobile play concept was introduced in the city of New York in 1977. The initial unit rapidly grew to a total of 59, operating from Monday through Saturday, with rotating staffs. Saturdays are, as much as possible, used for the staging of festival-type events with more than one unit assembling at a given site; during such days, each unit makes two different stops per day, holding two hour sessions at each site. A fascinating example of a festival session is the closing of Fifth Avenue during the holiday season. At that time, the entire street is turned into a pedestrian mall with mobile entertainment along the entire route.

The mobile units of the city of New York include, other than those that are similar to the Nassau County ones, a *Play mobile*, containing a playground directed at children under 10 years old; a *Zoo mobile* with a number of animals in cages and others roaming around while staff members, mainly consisting of veterinary students, tell the children about the animals which include monkeys, cows, lambs, goats, snakes, ducks, guinea pigs, parrots and rabbits; and a *Swim mobile*, complete with filtering system, heating unit and deck.

General observations

On the basis of the foregoing examples, a number of conclusions can be drawn relative to mobile play opportunities.

Mobility is their main feature and, irrespective of the service offered, it should never be tampered with. This implies that the unit should be as self-sufficient and autonomous in its operation as possible. Safety and organizational considerations, such as crowd control and space utilization, must have a high priority and therefore, barriers, street cones, barricades, emergency telephone service, loud hailers and/or public address systems should be integral parts of each vehicle's standard equipment.

Neighbourhood participation must have the highest priority in the preparatory phase of a mobile play program. Therefore, all efforts must be made to involve neighbourhood groups and agencies, as well as individual citizens in the planning, design and evaluation phases of the projects. This can be achieved through public meetings, individual visits, media announcements, and so on, culminating in the appointment, by those involved, of a neighbourhood representative as chief liaison between the project and the neighbourhood.

Mobile play facilities bring an important element of flexibility into the planning for play process. They can remain in one place anywhere from two hours to a couple of weeks; they can return regularly and thus develop a pattern, they can be used to provide additional attractions to festivals, play days, or other special events; and they are an economical means of providing variety in the nature and scope of services offered.

Because they lack the permanency of many traditional facilities, the mobile play facilities can adapt quickly to changes in fads, interests and preferences of their client groups.

The observation is often made that mobile play facilities, through the temporary nature of their involvement, fail to establish lasting relationships with the children; that their effect therefore is only incidental, that, after only a few hours they abandon the children, and that therefore results cannot be verified and measured.

Play Bus Rally – *Play Times*

Many of these viewpoints are valid; mobile facilities must *not* be seen as economical and efficient replacements of permanent ones. Therefore, the provision of permanent and lasting play opportunities ought to be the prime objective of those who are concerned with and for children's play; however, mobile facilities can play an important motivational role in reaching this objective. It is therefore important that a system of close cooperation between the two models be developed.

In respect to the above mentioned reservations, relative to mobile play facilities, one must furthermore appreciate that the stimulation, variation and interruption of the daily routine which the mobile play facility provides, may well produce experiences and impressions that stay with the child throughout its lifetime. The mobile facility can, from this point of view, play the same role as annual fairs, family feasts and holiday experiences.

One could say that the variety the mobile facilities offer matches the play pattern of children, which shows little continuity, but rather frequent changes and alterations.

As far as the development of lasting relationships is concerned, one might point at the family, kindergarten, school and youth organizations, all providing opportunities for long term contacts. It could be argued that free time contacts should be short term in nature to provide balance and harmonious opportunity to the development of independence. Mobile facilities play, in this respect, a similar role as holidays, the theatre, sport, movies, reading and museums.

Reflecting upon these conclusions, it becomes clear that the issue is not one of taking positions for or against mobile play opportunities, or one of mobile versus permanent, but that the issue is to strive for a harmonious development of both, utilizing to their maximum the positive characteristics of the two basic models for the provision of play opportunities.

Reference materials used in the preparation of this chapter include:

Schiller, Beryl. "R.I.C.E. – Remote and Isolated Children's Exercise, Inc.", in *The South Australia Teachers Journal*, Australia, June, 1979.

Progress Report – Remote and Isolated Children's Exercise, Inc. Port Augusta, Australia, 1979,

Jaarverslag, 1980, Brugse Dienst voor Speelprojecten, Brugge, Belgium, 1980.

Collier, Tom et al. *Mackenzie River Survival Project Report*, Government of Northwest Territories, Yellowknife, N.W.T., 1971.

Benjamin, Johanne et Silvija Ulmanis. *Western Report – Touring Museum for Toddlers*, London, Canada, 1980.

Ubersicht Kurzbericht Presse Echo, 1979, Pädagogische Aktion, Munich, Federal Republic of Germany, 1979.

Spielmobil, Infosammlung Pädagogische Aktion, Munich, Federal Republic of Germany, 1981.

Jahresbericht 1980, Pädagogische Aktion, Munich, Federal Republic of Germany, 1981.

"Bristol's Playbus: Just the Ticket" in *Play Times*, National Playing Fields Association, London, England, March, 1979.

Barlow, Cindy. "Off the Back of the Lorry" in *Child's Play*, Children and Youth Action Group, London, England, August, 1978.

"The Dublin Playbus – History of the Project" in *View*, Dr. Barnardos, Dublin, Ireland, No.2

20 Jahre Kinderzirkus Robinson, Pro Juventute, Zurich, Zwitzerland, 1980.

Wallach, Fran. *Mobile Recreation in Nassau County*, Department of Recreation and Parks, Nassau County, New York, U.S.A., 1977

Behrend, Cathie. "Mobility in Programming" in *Challenge!*, U.S. Department of Housing and Urban Development, Washington, D.C., U.S.A., March, 1980.

Children like to play anywhere and everywhere in their immediate home environment –

Children's Environment Advisory Service, Canada Mortgage and Housing Corporation

Playstreets

A s the title indicates, the purpose of this chapter is not to provide a comprehensive overview of the various spaces, such as public playgrounds, wading pools, playing fields and others, that have been set aside for children, but rather to highlight attempts to integrate opportunities to play into the overall living environment, based on the streets on which children live.

The decision to restrict the scope of this chapter was not founded on a lack of appreciation of the importance of these designated areas, but rather on a desire to underline the importance of integrating play in the overall living environment of children and a recognition of the fact that they do not make clear distinctions in time and space, but play everywhere and anywhere.

With the advent of the urban environment, children saw their opportunities to play progressively and drastically reduced; the street posed rapidly increasing hazards, the vacant lots disappeared and, for growing numbers, high-rise living eliminated the backyard. It is to the credit of those concerned with child development and its place in society that special places have been set aside to provide at least a minimum of opportunities for growth and development through play: play parks, play centres and playgrounds have become permanent features of urban environments. The need for creative activities and adventure were, to the extent that this was possible, met on the creative and adventure playgrounds.

In time, architects and legislators proceeded to include play opportunities in city plans and housing developments, resulting in a multitude of imaginative space utilizations where these had been lacking previously. However, the realization grew at the same time that, essential and significant as all these innovations might be, they tend to segregate the child from its total environment. Setting aside play spaces for children tends to have the same effect relative to the overall community. Children are set aside from it and live important periods of their lives in a segregated world, a trend that is reinforced in the exclusivity of the school world. For the modern urban child, the neighbourhood is no longer its playground.

Fortunately, all over the industrialized world, people realize that children are part of the neighbourhood and that the neighbourhood belongs to them as much, and maybe even more, than to the adults. Children do not break their neighbourhood up into a series of separate functions; for them it is a whole. They play it, always and everywhere, close by and far away, with nothing and with everything. They make their whole world into a play world, in the midst of the grown-up's world, which represents the parameters of the play world. Grown-ups are essential in this play world, just as playing children are essential for the grown-ups. Therefore, play cannot be isolated, but should be an integral part of the neighbourhood. One of the most rational ways to bring this about, especially in densely populated areas, where space is at a premium, is by using the street as a place to play.

Although a street consists of houses, a sidewalk and a main passageway for automobiles, populated by pedestrians, bicycles, cars, vans and other vehicles, a street is more than the sum total of all this. The street is also the place where neighbours stop and talk. The street is the place where people observe one another. The street is the medium through which the houses on either side are connected. The street is the place where each Saturday the ritual of the carwash takes place. The street is the place through which the drumband, the funeral cortège and the bicycle pass. The street is the space we go through to get from one place to the next. The street is the place where people demonstrate; where democracy is contested or defended. The street is traffic artery, meeting place, playground; the street is a multifaceted phenomenon.

But the street has also developed into a mono-functional automobile medium, severely limiting the freedom of movement of children, resulting in the functional separation of living and playing that we talked about in the beginning of this chapter. Attempts to remedy this situation, to re-create the opportunity to play in the street, close to the front door, without running undue risks, have resulted in the development of a concept called the playstreet. This is a street where one can conveniently and safely cycle, but also drive a car, walk, play, sit and chat. It is a street where one can look at flowers, trees or other people, meet friends, organize a party and do all those things that make living in a city pleasant.

The playstreet fits into the broader framework of the "live street" ("woonstraat" in Dutch or "wohnstrasse" in German); people live in their street in the sense that it is always there. They experience it continuously, whether they look out of the window or go out of the front door to go to the store, school or place of work.

A playstreet should contain pedestrians, cyclists, grass borders, front lawns, public signs, stores, benches, bicycle paths and, obviously, the automobile. To live and play on the playstreet means, above all, being there without danger, without concern and in peace. This does not mean, however, that cars must be banned, but it does mean that cars must drive slowly. The playstreet therefore, must have specially designed narrow spots and specific obstacles that force the cars to slow down.

It is important that playstreets be evenly distributed throughout the city, otherwise there is a danger of them causing significantly increased automobile traffic in the neighbouring streets, while at the same time attracting large concentrations of children from other areas. Creating a number of playstreets results inevitably in an overall reduction of the available street space for motorized traffic. However, this apparent disadvantage can, to a large extent, be offset by an increased use of the bicycle, and by growing numbers of people deciding to walk to the various shopping areas rather than taking a car.

In the following examples we propose to discuss different applications of the playstreet concept. These come from Argentina, Chile, Greece, Italy and the Netherlands. After having outlined these, we included a program from Switzerland in this category that makes use of an entire city for a specific play program.

Argentina

The Argentine *Playstreets*, taken from the municipality of San Fernando near Buenos Aires, follows the Greek concept described later. It too closes certain streets to motorized traffic, although only during weekends. The streets concerned are those adjacent to the city square, permitting the creation of a large play area in the centre of town.

The involvement of the municipality goes beyond that of simply closing a number of streets to motorized vehicles. Conscious of the important motivating role this instant playground has, the city fathers engage, for these weekends, a team of professionals in the fields of recreation, physical education and arts. They develop a large variety of activity programs, ranging from sports to crafts, fairs and games.

Although the overall program is aimed at the total population, special emphasis is placed on school children; the schools are encouraged to form teams in different activities such as balloon blowing, spelling, chess and soccer. These teams compete on Sundays and, based on the total scores obtained at the end of the series of competitions, the school with the highest accumulative score receives a prize from the municipal government.

Chile

In the city of Santiago, an experimental playstreet program, called the *Juan Vicûsa Street* program, was started in 1969. Jointly developed by the

University of Chile, the City of Santiago and the Chilian National Recreation Committee, it consists of a series of recreational programs for all population groups, developed in close cooperation with the residents concerned. These programs include the construction of a number of recreational facilities in the street, such as playing courts, communal gardens with vegetables plants, chess and domino tables etc. In addition, the organizers encouraged the creation of reading groups, crafts workshops and daycare centres.

Vehicle traffic was not eliminated but limited through the development of special transit schedules and circulation patterns.

An evaluation of the program performed in 1980 showed that the attitude of the residents to their environment had changed markedly: a much stronger feeling of belonging and attachment to the neighbourhood developed in the 11 years of the program's operation. A recurring problem however, and one that plagues virtually all community involvement programs, is that of securing and developing consistent indigenous leadership so that ultimately the people living on the street provide the human and financial resources required.

Decorating a playstreet

Greece

The Greek *Playstreets* vary from the regular concept in that they segregate playing children and automobiles — the Greek playstreets are closed to motorized traffic. There are, at the present time, some 150 playstreets in Athens, developed under a program through which the Greek government provides subsidies to municipalities which decide to create playstreets.

The concept is still new, which probably explains why it is only applied in a limited version that is commonly adopted in situations where experimentation with the playstreet is a relatively recent phenomenon. As is to be expected with all innovations that change a hitherto familiar environment, the Greek press and public have some difficulty adapting to the changes. However, the fact that the central government has decided to support the development of playstreets justifies the expectation that, in time and with greater familiarity with the concept, these reservations will disappear.

Italy

Although we cannot discuss a concrete example of a different application of the playstreet concept in Italy, we did receive a copy of a brief directed to a local government. When implemented, it will represent a unique approach to improving the quality of the total living environment. Developed by the "Verein für Kinderspielplätze und Erhohlungsinitiativen" (Association for Children's Playgrounds and Recreation Opportunities) in Bosen (Balsano), South Tirol, the proposal is a comprehensive one, in that it combines the playstreet with backyards to create a system of longitudinal parks combined with a *Network of Playstreets*. The parks will be created by removing fences that separate the backyards which will be developed according to a master plan.

If the resulting longitudinal parks are combined with playstreets, the expected result is an environment in which greater improved social contacts between children, and between children and adults, has become possible. Children will be able to play at their front as well as their back door; formal supervision will become superfluous because, as is the experience with other playstreets, the adults who live on the street will provide an unobtrusive, but highly effective system of supervision.

The Netherlands

A growing number of cities in the Netherlands combine two or more playstreets into *Woonerven*, residential precincts. Woonerven are residential environments where pedestrians, young and old, bicycles and cars, mix and move safely, because the woonerven are specifically designed for that purpose. All streets, old and new, alleys and lanes are potential woonerven.

The experiments started in Delft in 1971, and have proven to provide workable, realistic and effective solutions to some of the problems that threaten the quality of the residential environment.

A typical street before and after becoming a Woonerf – *Stitching Ruimte*

A typical street before and after becoming a Woonerf – *Royal Dutch Touring Club (ANWB)*

Frequently the tendency is to develop mono-functional solutions to problems involving pedestrians and motorized traffic, segregating both in time and place. Examples of the former are traffic lights, and allowing access by children and pedestrians to certain areas during specified times. An example of segregation in place is the creation of separate networks, one for motorized traffic and another for pedestrians.

The importance of the woonerf is its emphasis on integration of all users of communal space, motor-cars, children, cyclists, as well as pedestrians. The idea is to mix the different types of traffic in a balanced way, recreating harmony between pedestrians, drivers and cyclists and teaching them to cooperate and work together. These are the principles that have guided the development of the woonerven.

It is obvious that not all streets are suitable for woonerven; some are major traffic arteries, where the traffic function dominates. These could not be turned into woonerven without seriously disrupting essential services. Woonerven are therefore limited to those streets that have primarily a residential function.

They aim at reducing traffic danger, while at the same time restoring the environmental qualities of the street as a place to live in. Achievement of these objectives requires changes in legislation as well as in the design of the street. For instance, making motorized traffic less dangerous can be achieved by lowering the speed limit to one that is compatible with pedestrians and cyclists. This obviously requires changes in traffic regulations.

The Woonerf sign and the parking spaces are clearly marked and illuminated.
Royal Dutch Touring Club (ANWB)

To facilitate enforcement of such a compromise, the design of the woonerf can be changed in such a way that low speeds become the only feasible alternative. This can be done by creating irregular profiles, periodic narrowing of traffic lanes, shifting the axis of the street, etc.

Safety and visibility, furthermore, can be improved by removing the right of way of the car and giving it to all users, on the basis of "traffic from the right has preference" and by limiting parking to designated areas. By making crossing areas clearly recognizable, illuminating obstacles, and by ensuring that children coming from behind parked cars can be clearly seen, the design of the woonerf can favour the implementation of this type of legislative action.

The quality of the street as a place to live in can be further improved by adding elements with an environmental function, such as grass, flowers and benches, and by making objects and obstacles multifunctional. Trees, for instance, can be used as obstacles as well as providers of shade; pillars and bumps in the roads can be shaped in such a way that they can be used to play on.

Basic to the development of woonerven is the participation of the inhabitants in all phases of the planning process. The active cooperation and involvement of those who will be directly affected by the introduction of the concept is essential. Unless city planners, architects and developers design a procedure that makes genuine participation central to the entire process, the final product, not having the support of those for whom it was intended, will be doomed to failure. Participation in the planning process must include the evaluation of the project which, in turn, must apply to all phases of planning and not just the implementation.

In recognition of the popularity of the woonerven, the Ministry of Transport and Public Works issued standards, rules and regulations governing them in September 1976. This legislation stipulates, for instance, when a street can become a woonerf, which standard design provisions must apply to all woonerven, to their environments, etc.

The most important purposes of these rules and regulations are to ensure that those who enter a woonerf are fully aware of its nature and know how to behave; and, furthermore, that those who design a woonerf are familiar with the design requirements, so that the proposed woonerf indeed looks like one and can function like one. One year after the legislation was passed, about one hundred woonerven had been developed.

There are, obviously, problems connected with living in a woonerf. For instance, commercial vehicles making deliveries sometimes have great difficulty manipulating the various obstacles in the streets, and the many mopeds that characterize the Dutch landscape do not always favour tranquility. Living in a woonerf requires a good deal of understanding by all concerned and a willingness to solve problems in a human, responsible way.

Switzerland

The Swiss project we referred to in the beginning of this chapter uses one or two weeks during the summer and the entire city as a play space. It is the *Ferienpass*, the holiday passport. Its main purpose is to show children that the secret to a nice holiday lies not necessarily in far away places, but that their own city can be an exciting and fascinating place to be in. The project started in Basel in 1975 and has since spread to a large number of Swiss cities.

Its purpose is to provide holiday experiences to children and youth based on their city and/or neighbourhood; it should make establishments, agencies and events accessible to them, and be organized in such a way that they can use their own initiative and develop their skills, preferably in a game setting.

The holiday pass is the key to a new relationship with the city. It entitles the holder to a number of basic privileges such as free rides on all public transport, access to swimming pools, museums, etc. Over and above this, the city offers a number of special events such as playing detective with the police, climbing a tower that is otherwise closed to the public, attending various demonstrations, visiting industries, radio stations, airports, etc.

The holiday pass in Zurich, which can be purchased by all those between the ages of six and sixteen for 18 francs, consists of three parts: Part 1 includes the complete free package of the public transport system as well as free access to the city pools. Part 2 intends to familiarize the children with the professional and organizational infrastructure of the city. It includes visits to the museums, a printing firm, the street car depot, Swissair, etc. Part 3 attempts to contribute to the experience and activity level of the holidays through information on all that goes on in the city. Thus, it provides elaborate descriptions of all possibilities, recreation centres, sports events, visits to the zoo, libraries, etc.

General Observations

Playstreets and their various applications are typical aspects of high density living. They are, in most cases, attempts to remedy a situation that has developed over time: the onslaught of the automobile reduced not only the safety of the street, but limited also the available space; the growing popularity of high-rise apartments increased the population density, and the rising standards of living augmented the number of delivery vans.

Many projects like the ones we discussed in this chapter were therefore developed in older or high-density areas of cities. Modern plans for the development of cities, satellite cities and suburbs, increasingly contain provisions for the creation of playstreets, woonerven or other developments that recognize the child's right to play in its living environment.

The awareness is growing that, by providing separate play opportunities, we only meet part of the function play must perform in the growing process of children and that play should be possible in the presence of adults, stores, warehouses, traffic lights and the automobile. Therefore, the playstreet provides a comprehensive aspect to a play opportunity no segregated play space can offer.

One has to be aware however of the problems the introduction of playstreets may cause. Adults, who for years have lived in an environment where play was relegated to specially designated areas, often find it difficult to adjust to a situation where their exclusive domain becomes common ground. The inevitable noise and visual disturbances groups of playing children cause, require a level of understanding many older people often find difficult to produce, especially those who have no children of their own, or whose children have grown up.

Another possible area of conflict is the way in which the overall climate of a street changes. People grow used to their environment, even if this consists of noisy traffic, parked cars and other typical urban features. For a numbr of people, living in a woonerf-like environment creates a feeling of isolation, of being cutoff from the familiar hustle and bustle of the city.

Playing children may cause problems of supervision and discipline which were hitherto delegated to the playground leaders. A feeling often expressed was "all this is fine as long as our children are small, but where do we go or what happens to this neighbourhood, when they have grown up?" Therefore, changing a street into a playstreet, or developing a "woonerf", requires long and careful discussion with those who will be affected; it presupposes a serious, thorough program of participatory planning and real involvement. But above all, it requires the will to make it work, the openness of mind to approach problems in a collective way, and a firm desire to solve them. Playstreets do mean a change in one's way of living, for children as well as adults but, once entered into, they have the potential to give a new quality to living in a neighbourhood and thus to life in general.

The examples from Argentina and Chile are interesting because they show a level of government involvement beyond that of the more highly industrialized countries. While in the latter government support is limited to the provision of opportunities (for example the Dutch Woonerven or the German Spielstraszen), the Argentinan and Chilean Governments provide also leadership and organization for a wide variety of activities, thus creating, as it were, open air Community Centres.

Reference materials used in the preparation of this chapter include:

Melendez, Nelson. *Leisure in the Developing World: A Latin American Perspective*, paper presented at the Canadian Parks and Recreation Conference, 1981.

Speilstrassen, Verein für Kinderspielplätze und Erholungsinitiativen, Bozen, Italy, 1980.

Jonquière, Peter. *Woonerf. An Environment for Man and Transport Together – the Present Aspects*, Paper for the 2nd International Symposium on "Man and Transportation – the Future Aspects", Tokyo, Japan, 1978.

De inrichting van een woonerf, Royal Dutch Touring Club ANWB, The Hague, Netherlands, 1978.

"Fierenpass – Freizeitschlüssel für Daheimgebliebene" in *Pro Juventute News*, Zurich, Switzerland.

Kinder spielen Geschichte – *Pädagogische Aktion*

A Creative And Cultural Emphasis

I f culture, in its basic sense, is the way people "think, feel and behave", and if creativity refers to finding new ways of doing things, or organizing and applying that which is human in a different way, then all activities are cultural expressions and creativity exists wherever children play, gather experiences and interpret the environment in their own way.

Measured against these principles, this entire book deals with cultural and creative projects and there appears to be no justification for singling out a small number as being specifically cultural or creative. Acknowledging the validity of this point of view, we still decided to put together a short chapter on cultural and creative projects, setting aside a certain category that was specifically designed to bring out the characteristics that identify culture and creativity.

On the basis of this premise, we propose to discuss projects from Australia, Belgium, Ecuador, England, the Federal Republic of Germany, Norway and Venezuela.

Australia

In Australia the **Blue Folk Community Arts** Association Inc., located on the Strathnairn Homestead, operates the Strathnairn Gallery, a drama workshop and a theatre. Strathnairn Homestead was originally one of the area's largest sheep stations.

One of the major objectives of the Association is to stimulate interaction and creativity between and within children of all ages; the medium used is that of the arts. The following example illustrates, better than any description, the methodology used.

Although many of the specific aspects of the following play are rather traditional and appear in most daycamps, school art classes or campsite programs, its importance lies in its duration and comprehensive nature.

The children "live" a given situation for a whole week, developing their own norms and codes, learning to relate to others and to integrate their activities with them. This provides an environment in which imagination and creativity are used and developed to the utmost, and that it all takes place in a natural setting cannot but help enhance its significance.

The play is called "Dreams for a Sleeping Sun"; the actors were 56 children who enrolled for a one-week program. A good deal of the preparatory work had been done by the members of the Youth Drama Workshop, prior to the arrival of the children.

Basic to the play are five tribes, The Temple People, The Wardens of the Temple, The Lakes People, The Forest People, and The Artisans; the children were allocated to the various tribes in a very informal way. After this, each group went to work, developing its own village, legends, ceremonies, costumes and laws. They also made beautiful objects to decorate the temple. The artisans took apprentices from each tribe on a regular basis during the week and all took part in the creation of a huge papier-mâché Sun.

The Wardens of the Temple created a path of mystery leading to the entrance of the Temple; Keepers of the Fire made a large earth sculpture of the Sun and thus, the Temple grew in beauty and stature as the gifts and decorations arrived. The Temple people had the job of inventing ceremonies for the people of the Sun, as well as for the keepers of the legends and laws. Each afternoon, the tribes were called together in the Temple where turns were taken in presenting legends and dances which had been prepared during the day.

The week culminated in a performance which included parents and friends who participated, because they were formally registered in the scrolls of the respective tribes.

Thereafter, the Keepers of the Temple began their procession to the tribes. The Wardens of the Temple had completed the Path of Mystery, a beautiful, painted, plastic structure, running between trees and forming tunnels. Making music and carrying processional pieces made during the week, the procession made its way around the land, stopping at each village, listening to the music, songs and stories that had been prepared. The final ceremony took place at the Temple where each tribe planted a tree to mark the end of the dream.

The Association receives financial support from a variety of sources, such as the Community Arts Board of the Australia Council, the Committee of Cultural Development, the Department of the Capital Territory, membership fees, and, especially during the developmental phase, a number of service clubs.

Belgium

In Belgium the projects considered were developed by the *Centre d'expression et de créativité*, established under the auspices of the Service de l'Animation et de la Diffusion Culturelle of the Ministère de l'Education et de Culture Française.

The example related is that conducted by a group of "animateurs" in the village of Macquenoise, which is a village like many others. Its children play, build, discover, go to school; they are quite happy. They love modern music, gadgets and cakes; they spend their holidays in the village between homework and helping in the field; they know the rhythms of the seasons and take advantage of the sun as well as the snow. They don't seem to have many problems. They don't quite know what "animation" means, and they have very vague ideas about rural culture. They easily confuse video and television, music and Musak, painting and mish-mashing colours, creation and consumption, freedom and license.

The main motivation to work with the children of Macquenoise came from the realization that children of a village like that are limited in their development—throughout their lives they tread where someone else has gone before. The "animateurs" wanted to try to develop in the children the faculty for independent judgement, to teach them initiative and to challenge their creativity so that, hopefully, in their future they would be able to determine their own direction and make their own decisions.

The method adopted consisted, first of all, of discussions with the children on a large variety of items, as diverse as the high boots of American cowboys, Belgian folk music, the possibility of changing an area by using various colours, local sources of material (sawmill, grainary and the local glassworks), methods of decorating a place at little cost, etc. The next step was for the children to express the outcomes of these discussions in concrete action, in their own environment. This they did by publishing their own newspaper, making video recordings, visiting farms, playing a variety of musical instruments and so on.

By going through these consciously designed steps, the expectation is that the children's attitudes vis à vis daily happenings, and especially their capacity of adopting independent, personally inspired opinions and courses of action will improve, providing them with a broader scope of actions than they would have had if their only choice were to continue to walk in the footsteps of those who preceded them.

Another Belgian project deals with a theatrical experience with the mentally handicapped by an organization called CREAHM (Créativité chez les handicapés mentaux). Its aims are to promote and guide the development of cultural activities for mentally handicapped children and adults. The media used are: graphic arts; three-dimensional expression (sculpture, modelling); visual expression (film, video, photography); musical, theatrical and bodily expressions (body art).

Our example consists of a play created by the mentally handicapped. The emphasis throughout the presentation was on non-verbal expression; the actors were wearing masks, representing life-size puppets.

It was very difficult to interest the mentally handicapped youth in puppetry. They had great problems understanding the relationship be-

The children of Macquenoise transform an old shed with their creative talents   – *Michael Pion and Patrick Q...*

tween the puppet and the person operating it; learning the simple lines and expressing them verbally also posed many difficulties. The decision was therefore made to have the actors be the puppets themselves.

The specific objectives of the project were to bring the handicapped into contact with musical instruments, to teach them to coordinate their actions in time (for instance, one comes up, plays one's part and goes off, or one makes a puppet for a show that takes place much later), to develop non-verbal communication responses, especially by gestures, and to attempt to coordinate the gestures with the music. The method used was meant to develop an atmosphere in which the retarded and the "animateurs" worked together; the retarded making their own masks, building the stage and deciding upon the opening scene.

The first rehearsal took place with the entire group. The "animateurs" introduced the music and the actors came on stage wearing their masks. The only instruction they received was: "you hear the music, you wear your mask, you can do what you like". At first nobody moved. This lasted until the leaders put on very loud music; at that time people began to move. After that, the rehearsals took place in small groups. The entire performance was based on spontaneous expression; the involvement of the "animateurs" was limited to providing continuity.

This approach provided the mentally handicapped with a great deal of enjoyment and satisfaction. Learning to react to music, to express their feelings and to work together towards a certain objective has significantly improved the quality of their lives.

Another imaginative project developed by these Centres d'expression et de créativité dealt with colours. Children, coming from different countries, were asked which colours their country and their neighbourhood made them think of. They were also asked to identify colourless places. Next, the entire group was asked to put all these colours together and make a mural representing their neighbourhood. From this, they entered into a discussion about the functional role of colours, and the possibilities of changing an environment to conform to what they would like their neighbourhood to be. Through methods like these, children learn to work with colours, to express certain themes by means of colours, to change their environment through the medium of colour. Obviously these processes take many months to develop.

Ecuador

The Children's Culture House in Ecuador is a project developed by the Model Juvenile World. It is directed primarily to children of the less privileged sectors of the city of Quito, and aims at raising the level of understanding of the significant role leisure and recreation can play in the overall development of children and youth.

The means used are programs in arts and crafts, science and technology, as well as more general programs in the scientific and cultural area, such as visits to museums, planetaria, libraries, film libraries and audio-visual systems. The children attend in groups as part of the normal school program, or they come on their own. The centre is open every school day and during the holidays.

The facilities include a library, a theatre and a film studio. The activities of the library include, other than the traditional book-lending service, reading of poems and stories, reading of books to blind children, round-table discussions between children and authors or illustrators of children's books, and book expositions.

The theatre contains a children's theatre, where plays written for children are produced, and a puppet theatre with puppets, made and operated by children. The film studio deals with radio and television programs as well as educational films and discussions about films.

England

The Inter-Action Trust, London, has developed a number of very imaginative projects in this category.

The first one we want to discuss is *Community Alternative Poster Spaces.* The idea behind this project is to cover walls and other spaces in the inner city, especially those full of grafitti, with posters. The selected spaces are made available to schools, youth clubs, community groups and arts groups for the promotion of their activities or for creative work, such as picture displays, poetry posters, wall murals, stories, etc.

The public display of the creative expressions and promotional ideas is important because young people need places which are seen by many people where they can display their talents. Furthermore, many youth and community groups need inexpensive or free advertising space for their activities; from an environmental point of view, this project is an excellent method of combatting grafitti. It is also an excellent means of giving youth a sense of being able to influence and control their environment and a stronger feeling of belonging and ownership.

The preparatory work involved the selection of the sites, obtaining permission to use them, contracting the required materials, making the poster frames, installing them, and developing a system for periodically changing the posters. This project proved very successful, witnessed by the fact that there was a waiting list for poster space and the users of the poster method appeared quite satisfied. The project paid for itself through the leasing of advertising space.

Camera Kits teaches children to create and cooperate, to use new ideas and to learn to communicate these in word and picture to another group which, in turn, uses them to build on.

These purposes are achieved as follows: the children (not more than 12 with a leader) make up a story and draw it on frames on a roll of paper, much like a film. They then make a cardboard camera using large card-

Community Alternative Poster Spaces – *Inter-Action Trust*

board boxes with cardboard tubes for lenses; the "picture story" is now
wound through the camera and looked at by another group of children
that acts out the story.

The children are in the 6 to 14-year age range; the material used is
very inexpensive and consists of cardboard boxes, cardboard tubes, rolls
of paper (such as wall paper), and drawing utensils. This project was used
as a first stage leading up to pin-hole cameras, video and 8-mm film and is
therefore a good illustration of how play can be used as a tool to familiarize children with more sophisticated equipment.

Concrete Sculpture – *Inter-Action Trust*

Concrete Sculpture – *Inter-Action Trust*

Make-it-Yourself – *Inter-Action Trust*

The purpose of the ***Concrete Sculpture*** project is to develop in children confidence, skills, pride, creativity, and social responsibility by enabling them to make, with or without their parents, socially useful and environmentally enhancing pieces of concrete sculpture. The project often includes painting a mural on surrounding walls to provide a setting for the sculpture. The first such sculpture was made 10 years ago and similar projects have since been initiated in many locations around the world, under the training and guidance of community artists.

First, the children are shown a slide presentation or a film especially prepared as an introduction to the project; they are then provided with plasticine or salt dough to make a model of the sculpture they would like to make for the area that has been chosen. When all the models are finished, the children vote on which they consider to be the best one; they then help collect the rubble and proceed, under supervision, to make and paint the sculpture.

Another project developed by Inter-Action Trust is ***Make-It-Yourself***. Its purpose is to teach young people how to make a record, book, magazine or calendar and, through real game situations, develop a number of administrative, financial and social skills.

The project, scheduled over an eight-week period, is intended to produce a saleable product, providing the group involved with the resources to pay their expenses, buy additional equipment, or support a charity. An example is a production of a record of a school's musical with 35 performers. The entire group of 55 managed to sell five records each, guaranteeing £250 which enabled it to pay back part of the original production grant.

Make-it-Yourself – *Inter-Action Trust*

The group that decides to undertake the project meets once a week with project leaders, consisting of a member of Inter-Action, assisted by a local leader for the coordination of the project.

An independent observer attends each session and prepares an action research report on the project, while representatives from the Department of Education and Science, with Members of appropriate agencies, form a Steering Committee. The Department also finances the staff and training aspects of the program.

The planning process for each project consists of eight phases, including the preparation of a planning timetable, a feasibility study dealing with numbers and costs, the preparation of a budget, the procurement of a loan from Inter-Action, the development of promotional and marketing campaigns, the delivery of the material to the manufacturing company, the collection of the final product, its distribution and sale, and, finally, if the break-even point has been reached, a celebration party.

Projects like these are excellent means of providing young people with a sense of purpose, satisfaction and direction. They teach them, in an informal, relaxed and playful atmosphere, important skills, and provide them with a sense of pride in their accomplishment and place in their group and neighbourhood.

Another project, *Thematized Adventure Play,* developed by Inter-Action consists of creative variations on the adventure playground concept.

Starting in 1968 with the theme of Gulliver's Travels, the children constructed a 40- by 100-foot wood and canvas structure of Gulliver which, in turn, became the basis for arts, music, drama and sports activities, directly related to the Gulliver theme.

In subsequent years Moby Dick, the Trojan Horse, Dinosaurs, Batman and Robin, War of the Worlds, Frankenstein and Columbus became the themes.

Projects of this type integrate adventure play, practical and skilled use of crafts and arts, in a highly visible structure to which the children can point with pride. It provides, furthermore, an excellent opportunity to teach skills and issues through a literary image and to develop a creative activity. At the end of the summer the structure provides the basic ingredients for a large bonfire.

The Federal Republic of Germany

Kinder spielen Geschichte, (Children Play History) from the Pädagogische Aktion, was developed in Munich, Germany, for the summer holidays in 1976. It was an extremely comprehensive project, based on the history of the city, consisting of educational material as background for the performances, pictorial questionnaires, handicraft articles

Kinder spielen Geschichte – *Padagogische Aktion*

based on historical themes and miniatures, all leading up to theatrical performances by the children of Munich.

For instance, "Munich in the Middle Ages" was recreated from cardboard in a large municipal park. The mayor was a nine-year old girl; visitors came into the city through a "time machine" transplanting them in the 16th century; at the town's administrative centre people received passes and at the placement office they could decide whether they wanted to be a hatter, flowerbinder, goldsmith, artist or chronicler.

The town's watchman (11 years old) guaranteed law and order at City Hall and, thus, all functions were filled by democratically elected youngsters who, after having studied the history of their city from a variety of aspects, had little difficulty adjusting to their roles.

In this way, throughout the summer, the entire history of Munich was re-enacted and, indeed, relived by boys and girls between 6 and 14 years old. This project shows another, and extremely interesting, way to introduce children to the theatre and to their cultural heritage.

An interesting project is ***Tangible Theatre*** developed in Düsseldorf in 1976. It is meant to develop in children an understanding of the theatre beyond what they learn by passively observing performances. It wants to generate imagination and enjoyment in acting and performing, not only through the spoken theatre, but also in musical forms.

In order to reach these objectives, the theatre must present itself away from the formal stage; the children must be able to see and comprehend how theatre develops and how imaginative improvisations come about; imagination and performance must be tangible, within their grasp. Therefore, the Tangible Theatre has become mobile and goes to wherever the children are.

Upon arrival on the playground or in the recreational centre, everybody pitches in to unpack the bus which, with its fascinating contents, is a bit like Pandora's box. This experience of jointly setting up the theatre area is a very concrete and real one for the children.

In the next step the actors show how they play with the material and how they improvise. The theatre becomes a "lesson in sensibility"; experiencing the symbolic potential of the materials involved develops in children imagination and enjoyment in acting. After all this is over, everybody joins in again in packing everything in the bus.

The significance of this project lies in the active involvement of the children in the theatrical process. This aspect makes it stand out among the growing number of projects that bring the theatre to where the children are.

The realization that children's theatre should not just take place in a designated building is by no means new. Actors and educators have successfully brought the theatre to wherever children play, for years. For instance, the International Youth Theatre Festival in West Berlin, in 1978, included groups from Austria, France, England and Italy which regularly performed in shopping centres, schools and kindergartens. This approach not only strengthens neighbourhood work with young people, but it also makes the theatre accessible to children and youth whose parents are not interested in the traditional theatre and who therefore would never encourage them to go there.

Norway

The *Jebestuen Workshop* in Trondheim, Norway, is a project based on private initiative, conducted in part of a private home and large garden where children can express themselves, develop their creativity and satisfy their natural curiosity. The setting of the project makes it eminently suitable for the nervous and emotionally unstable children it wants to attract; the small scale of its operation provides a feeling of intimacy, of acceptance and of living in a family environment. Liaison with the community at large is established through visiting artists and local craftsmen.

One of the central aspects of the program is its spontaneity; there are no preconceived achievement goals and no clearly defined long-term objectives. With grants from the Norwegian Ministry of Family Welfare and the Municipality of Trondheim, the founders of the project were able to supplement their own resources and procure equipment, such as a ceramic oven, a potter's wheel, furniture and tools, as well as making the necessary alterations to their house.

The staff consists at the present time of a leader, two kindergarten teachers and two trainees; the children come in groups of 14 maximum. They draw, paint, model in clay, make puppets, and create theatre; they

Jebestuen Workshop – *Elin Host Esdaile*

build houses, boats, rafts or doll houses; they read, look at pictures, or study the theory of music.

The workshop is open every day except Saturday and Sunday, from 9 am to 4 pm, plus from 6 pm to 9 pm during the evening.

Venezuela

In Venezuela a *Children's Chorus and Dance Group* was developed by the Instituto Universitario Pedagogico Experimental de Barquisimeto. Its purpose is to use the relationship between school and society to facilitate the socialization process and to make a contribution to the overall pre-school program by teaching children to understand and value their neighbourhood, city and country.

The program was initiated in 1979, runs on a year-round basis, and is aimed at children between the ages of 4 and 6. The media used are those of physical and musical expression and the overall emphasis is predominantly cultural. The activities consist of Venezuelan dance and music and therefore requires, other than typical costumes, sound equipment and native folklore tapes.

The overall program has proven to be very successful; it provides extra incentives for the pre-school population, fosters interrelationships and contacts between the pre-school and the community, and enriches the pre-school curriculum.

Reference materials used in the preparation of this chapter include:

Mico, Domenic and Chris Rutter, *Blue Folk Community Arts Association Inc. Report*, Higgins, Australia, 1979.

Kinder Spielen Geschichte – Historiches Lernen in Stadtteil und im Museum, Pädagogische Aktion, Nürnberg, Federal Republic of Germany, 1977.

Kischkle, Martina, *Education for Creativity*, West Berlin, Federal Republic of Germany, Friedrich Verlag Velber, 1979.

Esdaile, Elin Host, *Report on Jebestuen Workshop*, Trondheim, Norway, 1979.

Reflections And Projections

L ooking back at the book we just completed, we cannot escape the urge to make a few comments that may help to "pull it all together", providing, as it were, a synthesis that highlights some of the book's main aspects and underlines some of the more important principles that emerged.

But we would like to do more than that. We also want to spend a few moments reflecting on what lies ahead; to pause and think about some of the implications of the concepts and issues we dealt with. We propose to project these against some of the major forces that shape the world of tomorrow in an effort to see more clearly their relative significance as well as the role each is likely to play in the universal quest to provide children of the future with the opportunities they need to grow up as people, able to live their lives to the fullest. In this process we realize that, as Roy Amara says in his articles on Futures Field[1], that the Future is not predictable, nor predetermined, and that its outcomes can be influenced by individual choices. Therefore, we will not venture into specific predictions, but rather attempt to outline and understand the influences on children's opportunities to play of such factors as demographic changes, altering norms and values, communications technology, work and leisure.

When looking back at some of the major conclusions to be drawn from the foregoing chapters, probably the most fundamental one is that *play is part of the human condition*; basic to human nature, and, therefore, universal. Initially we felt some reluctance to include some Third World countries in a book that deals primarily with play. We felt that possibly the over-riding needs for the basic necessities of life might have suppressed the need and concern for play to the degree that these had become almost trivial. The reactions to our inquiry, confirmed by the examples we have quoted, show that even in, and possibly because of, conditions of great physical and emotional hardship, play remains a fundamental prerequisite for human growth and development.

It may be that the *emphasis in the play experience varies*. The highly industrialized societies, based on efficiency and production and dominated by industry, science and bureaucracy, may have relegated play primarily to the realm of the child, considering that play for adults borders on the frivolous, having relaxation and compensation as only possible values. In the developing world, suffering from depressing economic conditions and low standards of living, play often has a utilitarian purpose. Recreation activities have to have a constructive objective and are therefore more closely related to education and economic activity.

We have noticed that many of the opportunities that have been created in recent years are in essence *reactions against the prevailing living conditions* in the western world. They grew from a desire to give back to the child the opportunities to explore, experiment, search, dare and create and are therefore typical for those parts of the world where these opportunities have virtually disappeared. It would be difficult to picture an adventure playground next to a tropical rain forest or a play-street in an Indonesian kampong.

They also form a reaction against the *highly competitive atmosphere* that has come to dominate industrial society. An interesting example of this is the history of the game of Musical Chairs we discussed in the chapter "Games: New Ways to Play Them". We saw how the competitive aspect was negligible in the 17th and 18th century when the game was called "La chasse au coeur". Participation was the principle throughout. The game changed with the mood of the time and became competitive: a winner had to be declared, one had to be the best. In recent years, through the efforts of the Cooperative Games movement, attempts have been made to bring the game back to its participatory origin — there is no longer one winner, but all participants are.

All modalities of application are strongly *influenced by socio-economic conditions, physical environments and*, above all, by the respective *cultural backgrounds*.

We have seen that the place of the child in a given society is a determining factor in the choice and nature of the play activities. In some countries the children's play world is the totality of their environment, whereas in others play takes place in specially identified areas.

Children in developing countries learn the main attitudes governing all social relations at a very early age. They are never left alone, often do not have their own bed, and, through contact with adults, they mature very quickly. In contrast to this, children in the developed parts of the world spend a great deal of their childhood years in the company of other children, either in daycare centres, schools, summer camps or social service agencies.

Participation by children *in the planning processes* is still *virtually non-existent*. In spite of a growing awareness of the need for this, planning is still done "for" instead of "with".The involvement of children in the implementation phase as leaders and change agents is much more widespread. This holds true especially for the developing countries where older children are given tasks quite early in relation to their younger brothers and sisters.

Another important influence on the application of some of the concepts is the *different time concept*. Time, in parts of the developing world, is still cyclical, which means that time passed is not lost but will come back, just as the seasons follow one another in a cyclical rhythm and just as life is everlasting. Therefore, one need not be concerned if a day has slipped by unnoticed and without one having accomplished anything worthwhile, because this day will come back and is gone only temporarily.

This concept is fundamentally different from the one that, since the industrial revolution, has prevailed in the western world. That world has been based on a linear concept of time, the basic notion of which is that each day that is passed is gone and will never come back. Thus, the purpose of life becomes to use each day as effectively as possible, hence notions of planning, accountability, efficiency. The modern production process is based on this principle; time becomes money.

As a consequence of this concept, life itself has become linear, divided into clearly distinguishable parts, each with its own rules, norms and regulations. We live our linear lives composed of childhood-education-work-retirement-death, roughly corresponding with the continuum playing-learning-working-nothing.

Cultures where the cyclical concept prevails do not look at life in this fractured way. Their distinction between the various phases is less clear and less artificial. Life is whole and indivisible. It is clear that such a concept is difficult to understand in the highly industrialized parts of the world. When each day comes back at some time, there seems to be little need for efficient planning and economical use of resources. Therefore, progress in the western sense would appear to be impeded.

Although these differences may seem to be fundamental, this is probably not the case. As the Dutch historian Jan Romein indicates, the pre-modern civilizations of medieval Europe and the developing countries of Asia and Africa constitute collectively one characteristic configuration which he called the Common Human Pattern (CHP) from which industrial Europe and North America deviate.[2] We are therefore not facing a difference in kind but rather one in degree. Realizing this makes it easier to understand a number of movements such as the renewed interest in the natural environment which, in essence, represents nothing more than a return to this Common Human Pattern.

According to Romein, the CHP man has a subjective attitude towards nature. He feels part of it, enduring rather than dominating it; his freedom of action is severely limited by the forces of nature. For him, life is not something to be realized by him but a gift of the gods, the spirits, or fate; death is only a transition to a different mode of existence. The CHP man's social, political and economic structures are based on traditional processes rather than being organized rationally. Authority is crucial, be it of the gods, the father, the teacher or the book. Authority is never questioned, it provides stability and direction. Essentially, the CHP man views work as a curse, as something one does if and when one has to, but which is certainly not a central life value.

The world of the CHP man is stable and predictable; social change is virtually non-existent. His place in the world is determined from the moment of his birth; he knows what his possibilities are, who he is and what is expected of him. In modern, western terms, he may not be free, but neither is he alone. His world is a secure one.

Therefore, the apparent changes in attitudes towards nature, the desire to live in partnership with it rather than dominate it, difficult as this change might be, does not represent an abberation, but signifies that modern, and more specifically western man, is returning to his true nature. The same applies to a number of other trends one can identify, such as the search for stability and direction; the search for and willingness to accept authority, albeit primarily of the charismatic type; the growing realization that we have gone too far in the movement towards specialization, cutting up the world of knowledge into so many specialties that people from the same scientific domain but different specializations, have difficulty communicating; and the emergence of holistic and multidisciplinary approaches.

The fact that the developing world offers a much closer resemblance to this Common Human Pattern is probably the main reason why the emphasis of this book has inevitably been on the western, highly industrialized countries. It is in that part of the world that man has deviated most from his real nature and it is therefore there that the reactions against his mode of living have been, and are, most profound and numerous. The western mode of living no longer provides children with the opportunities to grow up in accordance with their nature.

These reactions, representing a return to Romein's Common Human Pattern, will have important consequences for the place of the child in the society of the future and for its opportunities to play.

Alvin Toffler, in his latest publication *The Third Wave* has something interesting to say in this connection.[3] He foresees that society of the future will be much less child-centred than the present one. He believes that parents of the future will no longer live their dreams through their children, hoping that they will do better than they did and therefore investing large amounts of energy in them. Toffler, believing that this urge for socio-economic mobility will be much less in the future, argues that children will grow up in a world that is less obsessed with their psychological development and immediate satisfaction, but more structured, more limiting and less permissive. He also foresees that, as a result of the growing tendency to work at home, the children of the future will be much more and much sooner involved in jobs around the house and will have to accept responsibilities at a much earlier age. The result may well be a much shorter childhood, but one that is more productive and more responsible. Furthermore, since children will work much more closely with adults, they will be less vulnerable to the pressures of the peer group.

All told, Toffler foresees generations of youth that will be less consumption oriented, less drawn towards immediate satisfactions and less dependent on their friends.

When we consider these views, as well as the trends we discussed before, we realize that indeed, as René Dubos says "human nature is remarkably stable; its manifestations have changed continuously and will continue to do so according to environment and lifestyles".[4]

Therefore, if we now experience a renewed interest in nature, an urge towards interpersonal contacts, stability, direction and security, and if we attempt to create play opportunities for our children that will foster the development of these values, we face nothing extraordinary, but simply a return to some of the basic characteristics of us as people. Before continuing our discussion of some of the major forces that will influence the child's opportunity to play in the foreseeable future, we must point out the most significant and basic force of change and that is change itself and, more specifically, the *rapidity of change.* Whereas one hundred years elapsed between the discovery of the principle of photography and its practical application, it took only three months for the transistor to become commercially available; fifty years were needed to develop the concept of the airplane into a viable means of transportation, but only a few years to produce one that can fly at twice the speed of sound.

Although we know little about the process of change and, as Roy Amara says in a subsequent article in the Futurist[5], "very little about the role of images in personal or institutional change, how they occur, how they are related to continuous processes and how to anticipate them", we do know that the problems of adaptation to the accelerated speed of change have caused, and will continue to cause, serious emotional and psychological problems.

The impact of change relative to the subject matter of this book will primarily be felt in the need for highly flexible solutions to the need for opportunities to play; those with special responsibility in this area will have to become versed in the art of "projective" rather than "reactive" thinking; they have to be alert to rapidly emerging changes in personal and group values, lest they continue to provide opportunities that quickly become obsolete and, because of their rising cost of maintenance, probably counterproductive.

A phenomenon of great consequence for children and their opportunities to play will undoubtedly be that of their *rapidly growing numbers*, not only in an absolute sense but also as a proportion of the overall population. According to "Children in the World", a publication of the Population Reference Bureau in Observance of the International Year of the Child, in 1975, 36 percent of the 4 billion people in the world, or 1.4

billion, were children under the age of 15. If current projections hold true, this total will have grown to 1.9 billion in the year 2000.[6]

In 1975, 80 percent of the children of the world lived in the less-developed regions. The annual birth rates in Africa, Latin America and Asia were two to three times that of North America and Europe.

As a consequence, children under 15 made up 40 percent of the total population in the less developed countries compared to 25 percent in the other regions. The magnitude of this issue is shown dramatically in a statement made by Nelson Melendes, Executive Director of the World Leisure and Recreation Association who reported that, according to 1980 United Nations statistics, 42 percent of the population in Latin America was under 14 years of age and the median age in Brazil was 19.[7]

In 1975, about 800 million children lived in the rural areas of the less-developed countries. Despite an ongoing migration to the cities, the number of rural children in these regions is growing rapidly. One should realize that birth and death rates in these areas are higher than in the urban areas in spite of the fact that in 1975 some 156 million children in the less-developed countries lived in the slums and squatter settlements of the cities. Their playground is a world of open sewers and garbage dumps and their living quarters often one room shared with from six to ten other people.

That these developments will have serious consequences for the provision of play opportunities in those regions of the world is clear. One can only hope that the initiatives and vision of the few organizations and individuals we were able to report on will be multiplied manyfold to meet with the staggering need that must be expected in this area.

But, inevitably, this proportionate population growth in the less-developed parts of the world will have far-reaching consequences for the highly developed countries. *Migratory patterns* will change. Population increases through immigration in these countries have traditionally been from countries with similar cultural backgrounds. This situation is changing, and will change progressively. Already, countries of Western Europe and North America are receiving within their borders rapidly growing numbers of newcomers from countries with greatly different lifestyles, norms and values. One only has to observe the population of the average elementary school in a country like Canada to notice the change.

This situation offers splendid opportunities for cultural and emotional enrichment for resident as well as migrant. However it contains also a number of serious problems.

As Vincenso Arena reports in Der Tagesspiegel, "Migrant children are caught in a cultural no man's land".[8] The children of migrant workers in the Federal Republic of Germany have trouble with the language, experience difficulties at school, in finding jobs, and in their play activities.

Their problems stem from the fact that they are caught between two civilizations, two languages and two mentalities. They have to accept decisions that upset them and they are not always able to understand. The results often are anxiety, insecurity, even rebellion, and alienation.

An essential prerequisite for a solution to these problems is the development of an attitude of understanding and of tolerance towards those whose mode of living, culture and values may well be significantly different. Rather than reading about people from other countries, they now appear in growing numbers on the next block, across the street, or share the desk at school. We talked about rapidity of change and the need to adapt. One of the areas where this will increasingly be of prime importance is that of attitudes towards people of different cultural background.

Probably the most effective domain for this to take place is that of play. The informal atmosphere, the *traditionally classless* nature of play and the openness that characterizes the play world are attributes that point to play as the medium par excellence to bring about the harmonious integration pattern that will be so important in the future.

Another factor that will undoubtedly have a significant influence on the life of the child in the near future is the advent of what is often called the *communications age.*

Since the early seventies, the western world order has undergone a change from an industrial base to a communication base. One of the main causes for this fundamental change has been the "marriage" of the computer with the telecommunications systems.

This has resulted in a significant change in the world we live in. Whereas it had been characterized by industrial production, with its emphasis on consumption of energy and raw materials, the future communications society will be based on the creation, storage, manipulation and dissemination of information and therefore, the emphasis will be on communication. According to Porat, "the United States is now an information based economy... (in which) information activities engaged over 45 percent of the work force which earned over 53 percent of all labour income".[9]

Examples of the newly emerging communication services include computer publishing, electronic mail, electronic funds transfer, office automation, legal and financial services, remote catalogue shopping and many more. All these will have, and are in the western societies already beginning to have, a profound impact on our day-to-day living patterns, social interactions, work, economics, politics and leisure activities. We will see the emerging of generations of computer-orientated people and a whole series of hitherto unknown jobs.

This new communication age will influence the children of the future in a number of ways. The nature of certain of their activities will change through the inclusion of computer-based games; the fact that this new technology will reinforce the "work at home" trend may well significantly alter the relationships and place of the child in the family, and the instantaneous nature of this communication technology will undoubtedly change the nature of the world they live in. It is extremely important in all this to ensure that the basic human needs do not fall victim on the altar of technological innovations and that the interests of speed and efficiency are not served at the expense of the needs for interpersonal contacts, individual growth and development.

The expected impact of this age of communication will obviously vary from one world region to the other but, eventually, all will be affected by it and, if current indications are any guide, at a much faster rate than with any previous innovation.

That this will influence the *work environment* is clear. Here too, its impact will vary. It is clear that children will primarily be touched by the consequences of the changes in the work environment. However, attempts at humanizing work, at improving working conditions, such as replacing the assembly line with team work, sharing responsibility for production between workers and management, worker participation in the overall decision-making process and many more, have improved the quality of the work environment and will inevitably reflect on the environment children grow up in.

But there is more. Although communication technology, as any other technological innovation, promises to create more jobs than it abolishes, there will probably be structural unemployment situations as a result of its implementation. Whether or not these will be met by systems of work sharing, shorter workdays for all, longer holidays, sabbaticals, temporary retirements, or any other device, what is to be expected is that, for large numbers of workers, the near future will create a condition where there simply will not be enough work for all. Since this probably will not go at the expense of overall productivity, the general standard of living will probably not suffer, resulting in a situation where maybe not everyone has to work, introducing an element of choice. Here too, we seem to return to the Common Human Pattern.

That this will undermine the position of work in the centre of the value scale is clear. Consequently, other values, leisure in particular, will join work at the centre of people's lives.

Together with this we will inevitably see shifts in other values. Marilyn Ferguson has pointed to a move from what she calls the old paradigm of "protection values" like safety, comfort, image, self-control, permanence, power over others, adjustment, to an emerging paradigm of "growth values", such as spontaneity, meaning, authenticity, self-knowledge, potential, power with others and aspiration.[10]

All these will significantly alter life styles in general and those of young people in particular. Central to these value shifts is that of leisure which, as we said before, is moving more and more to the centre of people's lives. The realization of the importance of this move and the growing awareness of its significance to the quality of life will undoubtedly reinforce the move towards inclusion of leisure into educational programs. The educational authorities are increasingly realizing that the traditional educational principle of preparing young people for work has become inadequate, that children must be prepared for all aspects of life and that an important element is leisure and its opportunities for growth and development.

It goes without saying that a number of other factors will influence children's lives and their opportunities to play: the future energy supply, and especially the nature of its resources may have far-reaching consequences, economics will continue to be a major factor and politics will continue to play a role.

We did not attempt to be comprehensive, nor did we necessarily select the phenomena that will have the most immediate impact. It is clear that, given the different levels of development in the various world regions, the forces we talked about will influence life in varying degrees of intensity and that which appears to be near reality in one part may still seem science fiction in another. The purpose of these "projections" has been to put them in some perspective and to hopefully provide a forum for discussion and further study, which ultimately may lead to a better understanding of the forces that shape the future and to clearer insights for those who are concerned with the provision of play opportunities for children.

We feel that the trilogy we selected as the title for this book forms one of the prerequisites if we want future generations of children to grow up in a world in which it is more important to produce than to consume, more valuable to participate than to stand idle, more meaningful to create than to imitate.

Footnotes

1. Amara Roy. "The Futures Field: Searching for definitions and boundaries," in *The Futurist*, Washington D.C., 1981, Vol XV, No. 1, p.95.

2. Romein, Jan. "Het Algemeen Menseljk Patroon" in *Eender en Anders*, Amsterdam, Querido, 1964, as discussed by Anton C. Zijderveld in *The Abstract Society*, New York: Doubleday and Company, 1970, pp. 66-70.

3. Toffler, Alvin. *The Third Wave*, New York: William Morrow, 1980, pp. 229-232.

4. Dubos, René. *Choisir d'être humain*, Paris: Editions Desivel, 1974, p. 44.

5. Amara Roy. "The Futures Field," in *The Futurist*, Washington D.C., 1981, Vol XV, No. 2, p. 65.

6. McHall, Magda Cornell. *Children in the World*, Population Reference Bureau, Washington, D.C., 1979, p. 11.

7. Melendes, Nelson. *Leisure in the Developing World: A Latin American Perspective*, paper presented to the 1981 conference of the Canadian Parks/Recreation Association.

8. Arena, Vicenso. "Migrant children are caught in a cultural no man's land" in *German Tribune* Brussels, Belgium, Sept. 4th, 1981.

9. Porat, 1977 as reported by Dan J. Wedermeyer in New Communication Services for the Future, in *World Future Society Bulletin*, Vol. XIV, No. 1, Jan. Feb. 1980, pp. 1-7.

10. To appear in: Dychtwold, Ken and Villoldo (Editors). *Millenium: Glimpses into the 21st Century.*

Appendices

Selected References

Aufauvre, Marie-Renée. *Apprendre à Jouer – Apprendre à Vivre*, Paris: Delachaux et Niestlé, 1980.

Axline, M. Virginia. *Play Therapy*, New York: Ballantine Books, Revised 1974.

Bandet J. et M. Abbadie; *Jouer pour Comprendre*, Paris: Armand Colin, 1971.

Bandet, J. et R. Sarazanas. *L'Enfant et ses Jouets*, Paris: Casterman, 1972.

Bengtsson, Arvid. *Adventure Playgrounds*, London, England: Granada Publishing, 1972.

Bengtsson, Arvid. *The Child's Right to Play*, International Association for the Child's Right to Play, Sheffield, England, 1974.

Bengtsson, Arvid. *Le Droit de l'Enfant à Jouer*, Association Internationale pour le droit au jeu de l'enfant, Sheffield, England, 1978.

Bruner, J., A. Jolly and K. Sylva. *Play, It's Role in Development and Evolution*, Harmondsworth, England: Penguin Books, 1976.

Bundesministerium für Jugend, Familie und Gesundheit, Kinderspielplätze, Stuttgart, Federal Republic of Germany, Kohlhammerverlag, 1977.

Caillois, Roger. *Les Jeux et les Hommes*, Paris: Édition Gallimand, 1958.

Chateau, Jean. *L'Enfant et le Jeu*, Paris: Scaratee, 1967.

Chateau, Jean. *Le Jeu de l'Enfant*, Paris: Jean Urin, 1964.

Chateau, Jean. *Le Real et l'Imaginaire dans le Jeu de l'Enfant*, Paris: Jean Urin, 1967.

Demarbie, Andre. *Jeux et Récréations*, Paris: Berger-Levrault, 1967.

Ellis, Michael J. *Why People Play*, Englewood Cliffs, New Jersey: Prentice-Hall, 1973.

Elstner, Frank. *Spiel mit Deutscher Sportbund*, Frankfurt am Main, Federal Republic of Germany, 1979.

Erhard, Norbert und Wolfgang Zacharias. *Aktionsbuch: Mach mit in Zirkus Pumpernudel*, Ravensburg, Federal Republic of Germany: Otto Maier Verlag, 1980.

Fluegelman, Andrew (Ed.). *The New Games Book*, Garden City, New York: Doubleday, 1976.

Fluegelman, Andrew. *More New Games!*, Garden City, New York: Doubleday, 1981.

Garvey Catherine, *Play*, Cambridge, Massachusetts: Harvard University Press, 1977.

Groos, Karl. *The Play of Man*, London, England: William Heinemann, 1901.

Gutes Spielzlug von A–Z, Arbeitsausschuss Gutes Spielzeug Ulm, Federal Republic of Germany, 1974.

Harding, G. *Spieldiagnostik*, Weinheim, Federal Republic of Germany: Beltz, 1972.

Hetzer, H. *Spielen Lernen-Spielen Lehren*, Munich, Federal Republic of Germany: Don Bosco, 1975.

Hetzer, H. and H. Flakowsky. *Spiel im Familienleben*, Zurich, Switzerland: Bensinger Verlag, 1973.

Huisinga, Johan. *Homo Judens*, Boston, United States of America: Beacon Press, 1950.

Hurtwood, Lady Allen. *Planning for Play*, Don Mills, Ontario: Oxford University Press.

Kooij, R. van der und R. de Groot. *That's All in the Game – Theory and Research, Practice and Future of Children's Play*, Rheinstetten, Federal Republic of Germany: G. Schindele Verlag, 1977.

Kraus, Beat. *Spielecken, Spielplätze*, Basel, Switzerland: Lenos-und-Z-Verlag, 1979.

Lambert, Jack and Jenny Pearson, *Adventure Playgrounds*, London, England: Penguin Books, 1974.

Le Terrain pour l'Aventure, un Nouvel Espace de Jeu, Comité pour le développement des Espaces, Paris, 1973.

Leif, Joseph et Lucien Brunelle. *Le Jeu pour le Jeu*, Paris: A. Colin, 1976.

Limbos, E. *Terrains et Parc à Jeux pour Petits*, Paris: Ed. du Fleurus, 1975.

Mayrhofer, V.H. und W. Zacharias. *Aktion Spielbus*, Weinham, Federal Republic of Germany: Beltz, 1973.

McHall, Magda Cornell. *Children in the World*, Population Reference Bureau, Washington, D.C., 1979.

Millar, Susanna *Psychology of Play*, New York: Penguin Books, 1968.

Morris, Don. *How to Change the Games Children Play*, Minneapolis, Minnesota: Burgess Publishing Company, 1976.

Mugglin, Gustav. *A Chacun son Jouet*, Pro Juventute, Zurich, Switzerland, 1970.

Mugglin, Gustav. *Children's Recreation Activities, Facilities and Animation*, Council of Europe, Strassbourg, France, 1974.

Mugglin, Gustav und Alfred Trachsel. *Spielräume – Spielplätze*, Pro Juventute, Zurich, Switzerland, 1972.

Orlick, Terry. *The Cooperative Sports and Games Book: Challenge Without Competition*, New York: Pantheon Books, 1978.

Orlick, Terry. *Winning Through Cooperation*, Washington, D.C.: Acropolis Books, 1978.

Penninckz, Ludo. *Cours de Ré-Creation*, Confédération Nationale des Associations de Parents, Bruxelles, Belgium, 1978.

Penninckz, Ludo. *School Speel Plaats*, Nationale Confederatie van Ouderverenegingen UZW, Brussels, Belgium, 1978.

Piers, Maria W. (Ed.). *Play and Development*, New York: Norton, 1977.

Rouard M. et J. Simon. *Espaces de Jeux – de la Boite à Sable au Terrain d'Aventure*, Paris: Editions Vincent, 1976.

Sandels, Stina. *Children in Traffic*, London, England: Paul Flek, Revised 1975.

Savoie, Ph. *Terrain d'Aventure; Espaces de Vie*, Paris: Les Editions Fédérop, 1978.

Schneider, Tom. *Everybody's a Winner*, Toronto, Canada: Little, Brown and Company, 1976.

Spitzer und Günter. *Spielplatzhandbuch*, West Berlin, Federal Republic of Germany: VSA Verlag, 1975.

Ward, Colin. *The Child in the City*, New York: Pantheon Press, 1978.

Weschenfelder, K. und W. Zacharias. *Handbuch Museumspädagogik*, Düsseldorf, Federal Republic of Germany: Schevann Verlag, 1981.

Wilkinson, Paul (Ed.). *Innovations in Play Environments*, London, England: Croom Helm Publishers, 1980.

Wilkinson, Paul (Ed.). *In Celebration of Play*, London, England: Croom Helm Publishers, 1980.

Sources for Further Information

International and national organizations relevant to the subject of this book include:

International Organizations

Associacion Regional Latino Americana de Recreacion y Tiempo Libre
Compania 1312
Casilla 154
Santiago de Chile

Association for the Care of Children in Hospital
3615 Wisconsin Avenue N.S.
Washington, D.C.
20016 U.S.A.

Association for Childhood Education International
3615 Wisconsin Avenue N.W.
Washington, D.C.
20016 U.S.A.

Ekistics
24 Strat Syndesmou
Athens 136
Greece

European Leisure and Recreaton Association
Seefeldstrasse 8
8022 Zurich
Switzerland

International Association for the Child's Right to Play
12 Cherry Tree Drive
Sheffield S11 9AE
England

International Catholic Child Bureau
65, rue de Lausanne
1202 Geneva
Switzerland

International Children's Centre
Chateau de Longchamp
Carrefour de Longchamp
Bois de Boulonge
75016 Paris
France

International Committee for Fair Play
c/o Conseil international pour l'education physique et le sport
Maison de l'UNESCO
1, rue Miollis
75015 Paris
France

International Council for Children's Play
c/o Institute for Special Education
State University of Groningen
Onde Boteringestraat 1
9712 GA Groningen
Netherlands

International Council on Health, Physical Education and Recreation
1201 Sixteenth Street, N.W.
Washington, D.C.
20036 U.S.A.

International Federation of Park and Recreation Administration
The Grotto, Lower Basildon
Reading, Berkshire RG8 9NE
England

International Federation of Pedestrians
Passage, 61-111
2511 AC The Hague
Netherlands

International Rehabilitation
432 Park Avenue South
New York, N.Y.
10016 U.S.A.

International Union for Child Welfare
Post Box 41
1211 Geneva
Switzerland

International Union of Family Organizations
28, Place Saint-Georges
750009 Paris
France

International Youth Federation for Environmental Studies and Conservation
10, Rue Prosper Merimee
67100 Strasbourg
France

World Leisure and Recreation Association
345 East 46 Street
New York, N.Y.
10017 U.S.A.

World Organization for Early Childhood Education
OMEP International
Headquarters
81 Irving Place
New York, N.Y.
10003 U.S.A.

National Organizations

Adventure Playground
Raiffeisenstrasse 1
6000 Frankfurt 60
Federal Republic of Germany

American Adventure Play Association
P.O. Box 14782
Long Beach, California
90814 U.S.A.

**Association for the
Anthropological Study of Play**
Box 297
Alamo, California
94507 U.S.A.

**Association francaise pour
l'education par le jeu**
19, avenue Mozart
75016 Paris
France

Balkan-ji-Bari International
Ashram-Bapu Gaon
Via Dahanu Road 401 602
Maharashtra
India

Barnmiljöradet
Box 22106
10422 Stockholm
Sweden

**Bund der Jugendfarmen und
Akjtivspielplätze E.V.**
1, Elsental 3
D 7000 Stuttgart 80
Federal Republic of Germany

**Canadian Association of Toy
Libraries**
50 Quebec Avenue, Suite 1207
Toronto, Ontario
M6P 4B4 Canada

**Canadian Parks/Recreation
Association**
333 River Road
Vanier City, Ontario
K1L 8B9 Canada

Comite nacional de Recreacion
Los Lirios 389
Santiago de Chile

**Comite pour le developpement
de l'espace pour le jeu**
85, rue Saint-Charles
75105 Paris
France

**Comitato italiano per il gioci
infantile**
vis Jervis 24
10015 Ivrea
Torino
Italy

Danish Playground Association
Virkefeltet 2
2700 Bronshoj
Denmark

Deutscher Sportbund
Breitensport
Otto-Fleck-Schneise 12
D 6000 Frnakfurt
Federal Republic of Germany

Fondation Roi Baudouin
44 Pachecolaan
1000 Brussels
Belgium

**Handicapped Adventure
Playground Association**
Fulham Palace, Bishops Avenue
London SW6 6EA
England

Inter-Action Trust Limited
15 Wilkin Street
London NW5 3NG
England

Childhood City
Centre for Human Environments
Graduiate Centre - C.U.N.Y.
33 West 42nd Street
New York, N.Y.
10036 U.S.A.

Koning Boudewijn Stichting
Pachecolaan 44
1000 Brussels
Belgium

**Landelijke organisatie voor
speeltuinwerk en jengdrecreatie**
Nieuwe Herengracht 119
1001 SB Amsterdam
Netherlands

**Landelijke
Werkgroepkinderboerijen**
Instituut voor
Natuurbeschermingseducatie
Plantage Middenlaan 41
1018 DC Amsterdam
Netherlands

**National Association for
Education of Young Children**
1834 Connecticut Avenue, N.W.
Washington, D.C.
20009 U.S.A.

National Federation of City Farms
Inter-Action Trust Limited
15 Wilkin Street
London NW5 3NG
England

National Playbus Association
St. Thomas Church
St. Thomas Street
Bristol BSI
England

**National Playing Fields
Association**
25 Ovington Square
London SW3 1LQ
England

**Nationale Dienst voor
Openluchtleven**
Spastraat 32
1040 Brussels
Belgium

**Nationale dienst voor
speelpleinen**
15 Keiserslaan
1000 Brussels
Belgium

New Games Foundation
P.O. Box 7901
San Francisco, California
94120 U.S.A.

**New Zealand Council for
Recreation and Sport**
P.O. Box 5122
Wellington
New Zealand

Padagogische Aktion E.V.
Schellingstrasse 109
8000 Munchen 40
Federal Republic of Germany

Patronato Nacional de la Infancia
San Jose
Costa Rica

Pro Juventute
Seefeldstrasse 8
8022 Zurich
Switzerland

Sports and Games Cooperative
18 Bedale Drive
Ottawa, Ontario
K2H 5M1 Canada

Stichting Recreatie
Statenplein 1
Den Haag
Netherlands

Stichting Ruimte
P.O. 20732
Weena 732
Rotterdam
Netherlands

**Stichting Speel-o-theek
Nederland**
Sarphatipark 79-81
1073 CT Amsterdam
Netherlands

**Toy Library Association of the
United Kingdom**
Seabrook House, Wyllyotts
Manor
Darkes Lane, Potters Bar
Hertsfordshire EN6 2HL
England

**Verein für Kinderspielplätze und
Erholung**
L.d. Vinci Strasse 20/3
1-39100 Bozen
Italy

List of Programs and Addresses

CHILDREN'S PARTICIPATION

Childhood City Newsletter
Centre for Human Environments
Graduate Centre, C.U.N.Y.
33 West 42nd Street
New York, N.Y.
10036, U.S.A.

**Norwegian Institute of Urban
and Regional Research**
Brekkeveien 22/24
Oslo 8
Norway

Stichting Ruimte
P.O. 20732
Weena 732
Rotterdam
Netherlands

**International Youth Federation
for Environmental Studies and
Conservation**
**International Union for the
Conservation of Nature and
Natural Resources**
10, rue Prosper Merimee
67100 Strassbourg
France

**International Association for the
Child's Right to Play**
12 Cherry Tree Drive
Sheffield S11 9AE
England

For Every Child a Tree
**International Union of Child
Welfare**
1, rue de Varembé
1211 Geneva
Switzerland

**International Cooperative
Alliance**
11 Upper Grosvenor Street
London W1X 9PA
England

Architects-in-Schools
Educational Futures Inc.
2118 Spruce Street
Philadelphia, Pennsylvania
19103 U.S.A.

Met Open Oog Op Weg
Koning Boudewyn Stichting
Pachecolaan 44
1000 Brussels
Belgium

Better Britain Competition
Bennyrigg Nature Conservancy
Council
P.O. Box 6
Godwin House, George Street
Huntington Cambs. PE 18 6BU
England

ANIMALS, FARMS AND NATURE

Children's Farms
Nederlandse Commissie voor de
Cultuur van de
  Brusselse Agglomeratie
Hertogsstraat 33
1000 Brussels
Belgium

Riverview Park and Zoo
P.O. Box 449
Peterborough, Ontario
Canada K9J 6Z5

City Farms
National Federation of City Farms
Inter-Action Trust Limited
15 Wilkin Street
London NW5 3NG
England

Youth Farms
Bund der Jugendfarmen und
Aktivspielplätze E.V.
1m Elsental 3
D 7000 Stuttgart 80
Federal Republic of Germany

Jugendfarm Haldenwiese
Balinger Strass III
Stuttgart Möhringen
Federal Republic of Germany

Kinderboerderijen
Children's Farms
Landelijke Werkgroep
Kinderboerderijen
Instituut voor
Natuurbeschermingseducatie
Plantage Middenlaan 41
1018 DC Amsterdam
Netherlands

Speelboerderij Elsenhove
Bankrasweg l, De Elsenhove
1183 TP Amstelveen
Netherlands

Tolsered Junior Farm
GAKO Recreation Committee
Box 14034
S-400 20 Gothenburg
Sweden

For Our Own Development
Ridgetown Recreation Committee
Box 819
Ridgetown, Ontario
Canada N0P 2C0

Seeds for Self-Sufficiency
Save the Children Fund
157 Clapham Road
London SW9 0PT
England

Science Playground
Vikram A. Sarabhai Community
Science Centre
Navrangpura, Ahmedabad
38009 India

Service for School and Children's Gardens
Leidsestraatweg 77
2594 BB The Hague
Netherlands

Environmental Resource Centre
Old Broughton School
Macdonald Road
Edinburgh EH7 4LD
Scotland

Washington Environmental Yard
Washington Elementary School
2300 Grove Street
Berkeley, California
USA 94704
or
Mr. Robin C. Moore
School of Design
North Carolina State University
P.O. Box 5398
Raleigh, North Carolina
USA 27650

Children's Experimental Workshop
U.S. Department of the Interior
National Park Service
Washington, D.C.
U.S.A. 20240

GAMES: NEW WAYS TO PLAY THEM

Cooperative Games
Sports and Games Cooperative
18 Bedale Drive
Ottawa, Ontario
Canada K2H 5M1

Inter-Action Games Method
Inter-Action Trust Limited
15 Wilkin Street
London NW5 3NG
England

Spielfeste
Deutscher Sportbund
Breitensport
Otto-Fleck-Schneise 12
D 6000 Frankfurt
Federal Republic of Germany

Community Games
Cumbernauld and Kilsyth District
Council
Tryst Sport Centre
Cumbernauld G37 1EW
Scotland

New Games
New Games Foundation
P.O. Box 7901
San Francisco, California
U.S.A. 94120

BUILDING ADVENTURE INTO PLAY

**Harbourfront Adventure
Playground**
Adventure Education Concept
427 Bloor Street West
Toronto, Ontario, M5S 1X7
Canada

**Emdrup
Building Site Playground
Do-It-Yourself Workshops**
Danish Playground Association
Virkefeltet 2
2700 Bronshoj
Denmark

Lollard Adventure Playground
National Playing Fields
Association
25 Ovington Square
London SW3 1LQ
England

**Chelsea Handicapped Adventure
Playground**
Handicapped Adventure
Playground Association
Fulham Palace
Bishops Avenue
London SW6 6EA
England

Gan Hayaled
Society for Disabled Children's
Playground
P.O. Box 289
Haifa
Israel

**Bouwspeelplaats
Adventure Playground**
Zegvaartseweg 27
2722 PP Zoetermeer
Netherlands

Children's Scrap Centre
16 Burgess Street
Leith, Edinburgh
Scotland

**Huntington Beach Adventure
Playground**
Community Services Department
City Hall, 2000 Main Street
Huntington Beach, California
U.S.A. 92647

PLAY AND THE FAMILY

Time Out Program
Darwin and Districts YMCA
Youth Clubs
P.O. Box 1451
Darwin,
Australia 5794

**Familien Spiel
Family Game**
Pädagogische Aktion E.V.
Schellingstrasse 109
8000 Munchen 40
Federal Republic of Germany

Get a Family Feeling
New Zealand Council for
Recreation and Sport
P.O. Box 5122
Wellington
New Zealand

Pedagogical Play Centre
Jondal Sokneräd
5627 Jondal in Hardanger
Norway

Let's-Play-to-Grow
Joseph P. Kennedy, Jr. Foundation
1701 K Street N.W.
Suite 205
Washington, D.C.
U.S.A. 20006

Family Camp for Pre-schoolers
Camps with Grandparents
YMCA, Department of Camping
Techniques
Montevideo
Uruguay

Play and Learn Program
305 Rumsey Road
Toronto, Ontario
Canada M4G 1R4

Family Place
6560 Gilbert Road
Richmond, British Columbia
Canada V7C 3V4

One O'Clock Clubs
Greater London Council Parks
Department
Cavell House
2a Charing Cross Road
London WC 2
England

PLAY: A SOCIAL AND EDUCATIONAL MEDIUM

Outreach: Recreation Programs
for Remote Communities
YMCA of Darwin
P.O. Box 1451
Darwin
Australia 5794

Met Open Oog Op Weg
Walking Around with Your Eyes
Wide Open
Koning Boudewijn Stichting
Pachecolaan 44
1000 Brussels
Belgium

Children's Parks and Recreation
Program
Proyecto Recreacion Y Parques
Infantiles
Casa Presidencial
Oficina de la Primera Dama
San José
Costa Rica

Recreation Workshops
Ministerio de Educacion
Apopa
Urbanisacion M. Tierra 18a
San Salvador
El Salvador

Cuadras de Recreacion
World Association of Girl Guides
and Girl Scouts
132 Ebury Street
Westminster, London SW1W 9QQ
England

Book Bonanza
International Board on Books for
Young People
7 Albermarle Street
London W1X 4BB
England

Street Corner Children's Library
Boy's and Girl's Clubs Association
3 Lockhart Road
Wanchai
Hong Kong

Help Individual Scheme
Yang Memorial Social Service
Centre
54 Waterloo Road
P.O. Box K934
Kowloon
Hong Kong

Balkan-ji-Bari International
Ashram-Bapu Gaon
Via Dahanu Road 401 602
Maharashtra
India

Experience Workshop
Erfarenhetsverkstan
Box 3055
127 03 Skärholmen
Sweden

**Migrant Child Development
Program**
Gettysburg Schools
Administration Building
Route 34N
Gettysburg, Pennsylvania
U.S.A. 17325

Good Nutrition Program
Patient Activity Department,
Children's Hospital
Columbus, Ohio
U.S.A. 43205

TOY LIBRARIES: A COMMUNITY RESOURCE

The Toy Yard
Owen Sound Public Library
824 First Avenue West
Owen Sound, Ontario
Canada N4K 4K4

Toy Library
School District 43
555 Poirier Street
Coquitlam, British Columbia
Canada V3J 6A6

**Canadian Association of Toy
Libraries**
50 Quebec Avenue, Suite 1207
Toronto, Ontario
Canada M6P 4B4

**Toy Library Association of the
United Kingdom**
Seabrook House, Wyllyotts
Manor
Darkes Lane, Potters Bar
Hertsfordshire
England EN6 2HL

Ludothèque
Carrefour Chrétien Culturel de
Beaugrenelle
11 rue Linois
75015 Paris
France

Tricky Round Table
Children's National Foundation
Kamani Chambers
Nichol Road, Ballard Estate
Bombay 400038
India

Toy Library Service
Joint Child Health and Education
Project
75 Celicourt
Antelme Avenue
Quater Bornes
Maritius

Speel-o-theek
Brederostraat 35
8913 HE Leeuwarden
Netherlands

**Stichting Speel-o-theek
Nederland**
Sarphatipark 79-81
1073 CT Amsterdam
Netherlands

Venezuela Toy Library
Banco des Libro Public Libra
St José de Urbina
Venezuela

MOBILE PLAY OPPORTUNITIES

Tea and Sugar Train Playgroups
Remote and Isolated Children's
Exercise Inc.
P.O. Box 1729
Port Augusta 5700
South Australia

**Speelmanskarre
Playbus**
Brugse Dienst voor
Speelprojekten
Vuldersstraat 90
8000 Brugge
Belgium

**Spelleketrek
Playbus**
A.N.B.J.
Grétystraat 26
1000 Brussels
Belgium

Floating Swimming Pool
Sport Development Officer
Recreation Division
Government of the Northwest
Territories
Yellowknife, NWT
Canada X1A 2L9

Touring Museum for Toddlers
404 Victoria Street
London, Ontario
Canada N5Y 4A9

Mobile Units
Patronato Nacional de la Infancia
San José
Costa Rica

Bristol Playbus
24 Bright Street
Barton Hill
Bristol
England

National Playbus Association
St. Thomas Church
St. Thomas Street
Bristol BS1
England

Islington Play Lorry
2 St. Pauls Road
Islington, London N1
England

Kids Radio Van
Playcarts
Inter-Action Trust Limited
15 Wilkin Street
London NW5 3NG
England

Spielmobil
Jahrmarkt Spielbus
Spiel Aller Art Spielbus
Pädagogische Aktion E.V.
Schellingstrasse 109
8000 Munchen 40
Federal Republic of Germany

Dublin Children's Playbus
Dr. Barnardo's
244 Harold's Cross Road
Dublin 6
Ireland

Spielbus
Pro Juventute
Seefeldstrasse 8
8022 Zurich
Switzerland

Robinson Kinderzircus
Pro Juventute
Hofwiesenstrasse 226
8057 Zurich
Switzerland

Mobile Recreation Vans
New York City Department of
Parks and Recreation
830 Fifth Avenue
New York, New York
10021 U.S.A.

PLAYSTREETS

Playstreets
Municipality of San Fernando
c/o Professor Cutreras
San Fernando
Argentina

Juan Vicûsa Street
Comite Nacional de Recreacion
Los Lirios 389
Santiago
Chile

Playstreets
Ministry of Physical Planning
Housing
   and the Environment
Department of Playstreets and
Spaces
2 Panormou Street
Athens
Greece

Network of Playstreets
Verein für Kinderspielplätze und
Erholung
L.d. Vince Stasse 20/3
1 - 39100 Bozen
Italy

**Woonerven
Residential Precincts**
Royal Dutch Touring Club
(ANWB)
Wassenaarseweg 220
2 609 BA The Hague
Netherlands

**Ferienpass
Holiday Pass**
Pro Juventute
Seefeldstrasse 8
8022 Zurich
Switzerland

A CREATIVE AND CULTURAL EMPHASIS

**Blue Folk Community Arts
Association**
P.O. Box 46
Higgins ACT 2615
Australia

**Centre d'Expression et de
Créativité**
Service de l'Animation et de la
Diffusion Culturelle
Ministère de l'Education et de
Culture française
Galerie Ravenstrein 4
1000 Brussels
Belgium

Children's Culture House
Fundacion Mundo Juvenil
Avenada de Los Shyris-E-Rusiz
Quito
Ecuador

**Community Alternative Poster
Spaces
Camera Kits
Concrete Sculpture
Make-It-Yourself
Thematized Adventure Play**
Inter-Action Trust Limited

15 Wilkin Street
London NW5 3NG
England

**Kinder Spielen Geschichte
Children Play History**
Pädagogische Aktion E.V.
Schellingstrasse 109
8000 Munich 40
Federal Republic of Germany

Jebestuen Workshop
Jebeveien 5
7000 Trondheim
Norway

**Children's Chorus and Dance
Group**
Instituto Universitario Pedagogico
Experimental
Avenida Los Horcones con
Calle No. 64
Pueblo Nueva, Barquisimeto
Edo. Lara
Venezuela

Acknowledgements

M any agencies and individuals have assisted us with the preparation of this book. We gratefully recognize their most valuable and greatly appreciated contributions.

We like to thank more specifically all those who have shared with us printed materials in the form of letters, brochures, reports and books, as well as films, slides and numerous photographs. Their interest in the project, but especially their unselfish readyness to allow us access to the most varied information, have been a constant scource of encouragement for us. Although, for practical reasons, we were unable to use all data we received, it has all been extremely helpful to us and, without it, this book could never have been written.

We also want to acknowledge with gratitude the generous contribution we received from the Fitness and Amateur Sport Branch of the Government of Canada, which covered most of the costs involved in its preparation.

The World Leisure and Recreation Association, which initiated the project, has been very encouraging and cooperative throughout its entire development, and especially its Staff has been extremely helpful in numerous ways.

Our Canadian sponsor, the Canadian Parks/Recreation Association was not only instrumental in obtaining government support, but has been invaluable in its administrative assistance, especially Pip Moore, who spent countless hours typing and re-typing the many drafts of the manuscript. In this connection we also want to recognize the help we received from Lize Westland who volunteered to do the painstaking work of proofreading.

The International Association for the Child's Right to Play has contributed significantly to the success of the project by putting its extensive resource network at our disposal and, furthermore, we want to thank the National Forge Company of New York, and in particular Suzan Oostdijk, for providing us with translations of the Spanish sources, UNICEF for its encouragement, interest and support, and the Department of Recreology of the University of Ottawa, Canada, for providing us with additional office space and other administrative assistance.

Credits for cover photography

Large diamond shaped picture – *Robin Moore*

Left hand – bottom: Boy's hands –*Steve Bailey*

Middle – bottom: Children with horses – *Jane Knight*

Right hand –bottom: 3 Children-coloured faces – *Padagogische Aktion*

About The Authors

Cor Westland is an Associate Professor with the Department of Recreology, Faculty of Social Sciences, University of Ottawa, Canada, and Vice Chairman of the Board of the World Leisure and Recreation Association.

His experiences since his arrival in Canada from his native Holland in 1953, include that of Physical and Camp Director with the YMCA and Physical Education Teacher in a number of elementary schools.

More recently, he has been Recreation Consultant with the Fitness and Amateur Sport Branch of the Government of Canada and, prior to his appointment to the University of Ottawa, Director of Recreation Canada, a Directorate charged with the promotion and development of Fitness and Physical Recreation throughout the country. In that capacity he has had a wide international exposure, acquired an intimate knowledge of the various elements of the Canadian Recreation System, and was instrumental in the organization of conferences and study sessions on important aspects of recreation development.

Prof. Westland has served on the Boards of a number of national and international organizations, such as the Canadian Parks/Recreation Association, and chaired a variety of national and international conferences, for example, the World Congress of the International Association for the Child's Right to Play, in Ottawa, in 1978. He has published many articles, reports and studies in the general area of Leisure and Recreation and is a keen student of contemporary society and the forces that shape the world of the future. His facility in five languages has enabled the inclusion in this book of original material that hitherto had been limited to the respective language groups.

Jane Knight, as the national Play Project Director of the Canadian Council on Children and Youth from 1974-1981, was responsible for the development of the *Play Leadership Training Manual, Fair Play Codes for Children in Sport, Play Space Guidelines* and *All About Play- A Source Book for Planning Children's Play Opportunities,* as well as an annual series of multidisciplinary workshops and consultations on critical issues influencing children at play. Ms. Knight serves as an advisor to the Canadian Association of Toy Libraries and is one of the founders and advisors to the Children's Play Resource Centre in British Columbia. She is also a member of the Family Recreation Project and the All Children Play Committee of the Canadian Parks/Recreation Association.

Ms. Knight is the Vice President of the International Association for the Child's Right to Play and travels extensively in Scandanavia and Europe speaking on and studying the provision for children's play in housing developments, schools, hospitals, daycare centres, new towns and recreation-education programs. Study tours in China, Japan and other Asian countries have given her a deeper understanding of the cultural, geographic and socio-economic influences on children. Currently she is living in Paris and working as a consultant to UNESCO on children's informal learning and play opportunities.

Index of Play Programs

Play and the Family

Play: A Social and Educational Medium

Toy Libraries: A Community Resource

Mobile Play Opportunities

Playstreets

A Creative and Cultural Emphasis

WRLA, In Brief

The World Leisure and Recreation Association (WLRA) is a non-profit, non-governmental organization dedicated to improving individual and community life through recreation and the positive use of leisure. Founded in 1956, WLRA has been the leading international exponent for leisure policy and program all through its 25-year history. The initial purpose and commitment of the organization has remained unchanged. In recent years, however, there has come to be a much greater awareness of the scope, complexity and social function of leisure and recreation activities, which in turn has created opportunities for service that were not contemplated in the organization's early years. Broadly stated, WLRA's present objectives are:

- To promote an awareness of the significance of leisure and recreation in personal and social development.
- To provide a forum for discussion of global issues in leisure and recreation while fostering an increase of research activity in the field.
- To actively support recreation leadership development.
- To encourage and support the formation of regional, national and local leisure and recreation associations.
- To encourage the formation and development of national policies and programs on leisure and recreation.

Within this framework, WLRA is seeking to relate its specific activities to important developments in recreation affairs around the world.

WLRA's program rests upon four complementary services. These are: education, research, consultation and information.

In the interest of furthering these services, professional task groups have been formed.

They include:

The International Commmission for the Advancement of Leisure Leadership (INTERCALL), the goal of which is to foster the development in all countries of leadership training programs for leisure, recreation and parks at the non-governmental and governmental levels.

The International Commission for the Advancement of Leisure Information Exchange (INTERCALIX) has as its goal the fostering of exchanges of all forms of information pertaining both to an improved understanding of the nature of leisure in society and to the means of raising the quality of leisure experiences.

The International Commission on Leisure Research is now in the process of formation and its purpose will be to facilitate the development of new knowledge in leisure research through multidisciplinary and international exchange and cooperation.

A special ongoing program developed by WLRA over a decade ago is the formation of regional associations or regionalization. Briefly, this entails the identification of world regions that might have some parallels regarding leisure needs and interest and some commonly held beliefs regarding the solution of those leisure and recreation issues pertinent to the particular region. Pursuant to the latter, two regional organizations have been formed, the first of these is the European Leisure and Recreation Association (ELRA), established in 1970 and presently composed of 23 countries, and the Latin American Leisure and Recreation Association (ALATIR). Established in 1980 and composed of 15 countries. Regionalization efforts are currently underway in the Asian Pacific Region and the Caribbean.

The association's official publication is the **WLRA Journal** which is the only publication of its kind in the world. For 23 years it has kept the pulse of the international leisure and recreation movement reporting consistently on all substantive developments and trends in the field. A steady flow of professional input from our affiliates in more than 100 countries worldwide assures comprehensive reporting on relevant issues affecting our field and indigenous initiatives undertaken to address commonly perceived problems. In addition to the publication above, WLRA presently offers some 16 publications relating to international congresses, specialized directories and global reports on leisure and recreation.

Some highlights of service in the association's 25-year history include:
- Cooperative projects and activities with the United Nations, such as development programs in leisure and recreation for refugees in the Middle-East and Asia.
- Preparation of a global status report on Leisure and Recreation in Human Settlements for the UN Habitat Conference, out of which resolution C.18 emanated. This resolution establishes that the right to leisure and recreation is a basic human need.
- A program of exchanges for professionals in the field geared to enhancing their technical competence was instituted in 1957 and to this day remains a worthwhile effort. Over the years, it has involved over 500 professionals in more than 60 countries.
- Consistent with its purposes, the association has been instrumental in the organisation of more than 20 national recreational organizations throughout its 25-year history.

- Has provided field services in leadership development, direct consultation to governments and other national organizations and provided Ad Hoc services such as temporary delivery of recreation programs in more than 50 countries throughout the world.
- The Association has sponsored and co-sponsored a great many regional and world congresses in the field starting with the first World Recreation Congress held in Japan in 1965. Some recent such activities include the first European Recreation Congress at Geneva, the workshop on Leisure and Recreation in Human Settlements, Habitat Conference in Canada, the first International Conference on Advancement for Leadership for Leisure in Michigan, the second World Congress on Development of Leadership for Leisure in Puerto Rico, the first Latin American Symposium on Non-formal Education Through Recreation in Venezuela, the first International Leisure Information Network Conference in Brussels.
- In the mid-70's the association created the Tom and Ruth Rivers Scholarship with the intent of exposing students to the rich flow of technical information available at the different international and national congresses on leisure and recreation. More than 30 students have participated since the scholarship's inception.
- Developed after 2 ½ years of work, **the charter for leisure** in the interest of offering worldwide guidance regarding planning for leisure and recreational services.

For more specific information on highlights of service during the association's quarter century of existence, please refer to Volume XXIII, Issues 1 thru 5 of the WLRA Journal.

IPA Declaration of the Child's Right to Play

Prepared for International Year of the Child at an international consultation in Malta hosted by the International Association for the Childs' Right to Play (Formerly the International Playground Association).

The Malta Consultation declares that play, along with the basic needs of nutrition, health, shelter and education, is vital for the development of the potential of all children.

The child is the foundation for the world's future.

Play is not the mere passing of time. Play is life.

It is instinctive. It is voluntary. It is spontaneous. It is natural. It is exploratory. It is commmunication. It is expression. It combines action and thought. It gives satisfaction and a feeling of achievement.

Play has occurred at all times throughout history and in all cultures. Play touches all aspects of life.

Through play the child develops physically, mentally, emotionally and socially.

Play is a means of learning to live.

The Consultation is extremely concerned by a number of alarming trends, such as:

- Society's indifference to the importance of play.
- The over-emphasis on academic studies in schools.
- The dehumanising scale of settlements, inappropriate housing forms; such as high-rise, inadequate environmental planning and bad traffic management.
- The increasing commercial exploitation of children through mass communication, mass production, leading to the deterioration of individual values and cultural tradition.
- The inadequate preparation of children to live in a rapidly changing society.

Proposals for Action

Health

Play is essential for the physical and mental health of the child.
- Establish programmes for professionals and parents about the benefits of play from birth onwards.
- Incorporate play into community programmes designed to maintain the child's health.
- Promote play as an integral part of the treatment plan for children in hospitals and other settings.

Education

Play is part of education for life.
- Provide opportunities for initiative, interaction, creativity and socialisation in the formal education system.
- Include the study of the importance of play in the training of all professionals working with or for children.
- Involve schools, colleges and public buildings in the life of the community and permit fuller use of these buildings and facilities.

Welfare

Play is an essential part of family and community welfare.
- Promote measures that strengthen the close relationship between parent and child.
- Ensure that play is accepted as an integral part of social development and social care.
- Provide community based services of which play is a part in order to foster the acceptance of children with handicaps as full members of the community so that no child, whether for physical, mental or emotional reasons shall be detained in an institution.

Leisure

The child needs time to play.
- Provide the space and adequate free time for children to choose and develop individual and group interests.
- Encourage more people from different backgrounds and ages to be involved with children.
- Stop the commercial exploitation of children's play, e.g. manipulative advertising, war toys and violence in entertainment.

Planning

The child must have priority in the planning of human settlements.
- Give priority to the child in existing and projected human settlements in view of the child's great vulnerability, small size and limited range of activity.
- Ban immediately the building of all high-rise housing and take urgent steps to mitigate the effect of existing developments on children.
- Take steps to enable the child to move about the community in safety by providing traffic segregation, improved public transportation and better traffic management.

The Malta Consultation

- Believing firmly that the International Year of the Child will provide opportunities to arouse world opinion for the improvement of the life of the child.
- Affirming its belief in the United Nations' Declaration of the Rights of the Child.
- Acknowledging that each country is responsible for preparing its own courses of action in the lights of its culture, climate and social, political and economic structure.
- Recognizing that the full participation of people is essential in planning and developing programmes and services for children to meet their needs, wishes and aspirations.
- Assuring its co-operation with other international and national organisations involved with children.

Appeals to all countries and organisations to consider seriously the implementation of measures to reverse the alarming trends, some of which are identified in this statement, and to place high on its list of priorities the development of long term programmes to ensure for all time

The Child's Right to Play.

The UN General Assembly Meeting in December 1976 declared 1979 as the International Year of the Child.

The UNO Declaration of the Rights of the Child says in Article 7 "The Child shall have full opportunity to play and recreation which should be directed to the same purpose as education".

IPA the International Association for the Child's Right to Play is an inter-disciplinary organisation recognised by the United Nations Economic and Social Council, UNESCO and by UNESCO as a non-governmental organisation with consultative status.

International Association for the Child's
Right to Play
IPA, 12 Cherry Tree Drive,
Sheffield, S11 9AE, U.K.
Copies of the report of the Consultation can be obtained from IPA.

211